TOWARDS THE DAWN

Clifford Hill is both a sociologist and a theologian.
Known internationally for his writings and broad-
cast work in race relations, his contribution in this
field is based on the personal experience of living
and working in a multi-racial community in the East
End of London, where he founded the Newham
Community Renewal Programme. He was also a co-
founder of the Martin Luther King Foundation. He
has been a senior lecturer in Sociology in the University of London, specializing in the Sociology of
Religion, and a part-time lecturer at Spurgeon's
Theological College, as well as examiner in Divinity
of the University of London Institute of Education.

Dr Hill is an ordained minister in the Congre-
gational Church and was national President 1976/7
He is now directing the national interdenomina-
tional evangelism movement 'New Way', sponsored
by the Evangelical Alliance.

TOWARDS THE DAWN

You know what hour it is, how it is full time now for you to wake from sleep. For salvation is nearer to us now than when we first believed.

The night is far gone, the day is at hand. Let us then cast off the works of darkness and put on the armour of light.

Romans 13:11 and 12

CLIFFORD HILL

TOWARDS THE DAWN

What is happening to Britain today?

Collins
FOUNT PAPERBACKS

First published in 1980 by
Fount Paperbacks, London
Third Impression August 1982

© Clifford Hill 1980

Made and printed in Great Britain by
William Collins Sons & Co. Ltd, Glasgow

BIBLE REFERENCES

Except where otherwise noted, all Bible references
are taken from the *Revised Standard Version:
Common Bible* © Copyright 1973 by the Division
of Education of the National Council of the
Churches of Christ in the United States of America,
published in New York, Glasgow and Toronto by
William Collins Sons & Co Ltd.

CONTENTS

AUTHOR'S PREFACE

To write this book has been one of the strangest experiences of my life. It began about four years ago when I was lecturing at Spurgeon's College. I was speaking on the social structure of modern Britain, analysing the forces of social change, when I suddenly found myself being completely carried away from my notes. I began to tingle with excitement in the same way as occasionally happens when I'm preaching or privately at prayer. I knew I was being given a revelation of divine truth but it seemed almost unbelievable that it should happen during a sociology lecture – even in a Baptist theological college!

The strong sense of the presence of God guiding my thinking remained with me and for three days and nights I hardly left my study, examining what I had seen both Biblically and in terms of sociological theory. I began to work it into the format of a book but was very clearly stopped. About a year later I tried again and actually completed two chapters before being stopped once more, and this time I was very clearly told that the time was not yet right but that I would be shown when to write.

The following year I left the East End of London and plunged into a new and wider world as I travelled the country in preparation for leading the Decade of Evangelism. Any thoughts of writing soon faded into the background as I began to fulfil a hectic round of speaking engagements, committees and organizational duties. Then, early in 1979 I was due to lead a day retreat at the London Bible College for the staff of British Youth for Christ. The day began with Bible study led by the Rev Barry Kissell of St Andrew's Parish Church, Chorley Wood. I had never spoken to him in my life, although I remembered having seen him a few months earlier, across the room at a committee.

After his session we had a coffee break before I was due to speak. In the corridor outside the lecture room Barry stopped me and said, 'I've got a message for you.' I looked at him in mild surprise wondering whom he knew who also knew me. I said, 'Who's it from?' and he said, 'It's from the Lord.'

I stood rooted to the spot. In the radical social-action sector of the Church in which I had been educated and had worked for most of my life, you didn't get messages from the Lord! Indeed I had always despised those Christians I had denigrated as having 'a hot line to God'. I found myself staring dumbly at him, but Barry continued unperturbed, 'I was at prayer yesterday when you came into my mind and the Lord gave me a message for you. I didn't know I was going to see you today so I've written to you.' In fact, he said, 'I posted it on the way here this morning. You'll get a letter from me tomorrow.'

'Oh yes,' I said dully. 'What's the message?' 'It's this,' ne said opening his Bible at Habakkuk chapter 2 and verse 2: 'Write down clearly what I reveal to you so that it may be read at a glance. Put it in writing because it is not yet time for it to come true. But the time is coming quickly and what I show you will come true. It may seem slow in coming but wait for it: it will certainly take place and it will not be long delayed.

'I don't know what it means,' Barry continued, 'but that's the message.' I reeled as though receiving a physical blow in the pit of the stomach, pulled myself together, stammered my thanks and left him to try to concentrate my thoughts on leading the day retreat. I have not seen or spoken to Barry again since then, and up to the time of writing this preface he still does not know the significance of that message.

But although I knew God was warning me that the time was near to begin writing, there was one more thing that had to happen first. There were things wrong in my life, and in particular I had to be broken of the pride of self-confidence that had always been a part of my nature. I was going through a period of intense personal trouble, and God used this to break me and fill me with the power I had always yearned for but never possessed. Christians will understand what I mean if I say that the line of the little chorus 'Break me, melt me, mould me, fill me' was fulfilled in my life. God often uses the times of personal suffering as the anvil on which he hammers out the new man.

I knew now that the time of writing was very close and I simply had to await the opportunity in a heavily crammed diary. It came just as unexpectedly when a couple of months later, in the summer of 1979, a virus left me with a throat infection that forced me to cancel all meetings for a month. When I began to write this time what came was a completely fresh approach. Once the task was begun I hardly stopped day and night for four weeks. The result is not a text book studded with references to scholarly works. It was not written as a cold academic study.

I believe it to be a message from God to our nation at a time when the world is plunging into recession, when the foundations of Western civilization are crumbling, and when the nations are stumbling towards the most destructive war in the history of mankind. Let he who has ears to hear, hear what the Lord has to say to this land.

I acknowledge with gratitude my indebtedness to Monica, my wife, who has shared in my spiritual journey and whose specialized knowledge of the Church Growth field has contributed much to my thinking, especially in chapter 5. I also wish to express gratitude to the Very Rev David Edwards and the Rev Pat Dearnley for helpful comments on the draft manuscript, and to Margaret Chilver, Beryl English and Eileen Richardson for dedicated work in producing the typescript, also to Messrs William Collins for the incredible speed with which they have produced this book.

January 1980   CLIFFORD HILL

THE
PROPHETIC TASK

Where there is no vision, the people perish.
Proverbs 29:18
(Authorized Version)

CHAPTER ONE

THE PROPHETIC TASK

The most urgent need in Britain today is for the recovery of the authentic voice of prophecy in the life of the nation. Historically this has been the task not simply of individuals but of the Church as the corporate body of Christ through its faithful witness to the truth and fearless preaching of the Gospel. There have been times when that witness has been extremely powerful and influential in the life of the nation and there have been times when it has been very weak. We are at present in a period when the prophetic voice has been almost silent and unheard in Britain for many years. There have been individual voices but they have either been ignored or their words have gone unheeded. Prophecy does not involve simply foretelling the future. It is primarily a witness to the truth. It stands for the enunciation of fundamental values such as love, justice and truth. It applies the unchanging word of God to the changing circumstances of man.

Historically the prophetic task stems from the great prophetic tradition in the religion of Israel. From the time of Joshua – who faced the nation with the choice between serving the God of their fathers, Abraham and Isaac, and the Baalim or false gods of the surrounding nations – the ideal for Israel was to order the whole of her national life according to the word and will of God. His will was made known and interpreted to the nation in each generation through the prophets. Theirs was the twofold task of being 'holy unto the Lord', i.e. maintaining a degree of separation from the ordinary common things of life in order to live really close to God and to be conscious of his presence and therefore able to be his mouthpiece; and secondly of being sufficiently close and in touch with the ordinary everyday events of life, so as to be able to discern the signs of the times and thereby to interpret the word of God to the life of the nation.

There were two types of prophet in ancient Israel.[1] There were the 'bands of prophets' and there were the individual men of God. These are sometimes known as the 'Nebiim' and the 'Canonical prophets'. The former are usually charac- terized by ecstasy and emotion, and were often in wandering bands or associated with cultic practices. They were the 'pro- fessional' prophets who sometimes appeared to have more in common with the culture of the people than with the word of God. There were times when they became mixed up with the polytheistic practices (the Baalim) of the tribal peoples amongst whom the Jews had settled in central Palestine, as in the time of Ahab and Jezebel. There were other times when they simply represented the *vox populi*, as when Jehoshaphat was not satisfied with the advice of the four hundred prophets who unanimously advised him to go into battle against Syria. He sent for the individual man of God, Micaiah, who advised against the conflict (2 Chronicles 18:4–22).

The individual man of God was the second type of prophet in Old Testament tradition. He stood at the heart of the 'holiness' tradition of ancient Israel, which stemmed from the Covenant established with Abraham and sealed through the prophetic ministry of Moses. The great eighth- to sixth- century prophets who brought the word of God to the nation in days of social, political, moral and spiritual crisis were often lone voices. The word they brought was often highly un- popular and sometimes even considered unpatriotic, but they represented the epitome of the true religion of Israel.

It is this strand of prophecy with which we are concerned in this book. There were four outstanding characteristics of the prophet who stood both within the mainstream of religious purity and for absolute obedience to the word of God. They are:

(1) He was first and foremost conscious of the presence of God. He was a man who was in constant communication with God. He spoke with God and God spoke with him.

(2) Secondly, he was a man under authority. He did not offer his own opinions or personal views on a subject. He was a servant of God, under his authority and obedient to him, so that when the prophet spoke he brought the authoritative word of God. He said 'thus says the Lord'. He was the mouthpiece of God to relay his word to the nation.

(3) Thirdly, he was a man with a spirit of discernment. This was a gift from God, part of the essential equipment of the prophet. He had the ability to discern good and evil, to read the signs of the times, to understand the social, political and economic, as well as the spiritual, state of the nation. He was thus in a position to interpret the word of God to the needs of the nation.

(4) Fourthly, he had power. He did not possess power in an earthly or human sense. He was not a rich man, a ruler, a politician or a priest, but neither was he an ordinary citizen. He had been called by God to a specific task, therefore he was 'holy unto the Lord'. He was filled with the power of God's Spirit. When he spoke, the word of God was communicated with power to his hearers.

These four characteristics of the prophet can be seen as the genuine hallmarks of the prophetic role in every generation. The great prophets of each century were clearly marked out as men of God. They made a tremendous impact upon the life of the nation as they transmitted the word of God to meet the needs of the people against the background of the social and political conditions of the day. In the New Testament the Apostles were clearly men in whom the presence of the risen Christ was a living reality. The Holy Spirit was upon them and they spoke the word of the Lord with authority and power. The same is true of the great preachers and writers in the Christian Church down the centuries. Each of them has been a man upon whom God has bestowed power and authority, yet a power and authority not derived from human sources, but coming from the word of God and the inspiration of the Holy Spirit. The prophetic task is to use in the life of the nation that God-given wisdom and insight into the lives of people and into the great issues of the day. It is a wisdom and insight that derives from a constant openness to God, living in the presence of the Lord and through constant study of the scriptures. Thus the prophetic task is to bring the word of the Lord to bear in each generation upon the great issues of the day in the national life.

The prophetic task is not an easy one. It is, in fact, the most onerous task in the world because it carries such enormous responsibility. Those who exercise a prophetic ministry must be prepared for suffering. They will meet fierce opposition, ridicule and contempt from those who hate to hear God speaking to them, and refuse to accept his message. Men have always preferred darkness to light. They do not wish their evil deeds to be brought to the light, so they have resisted the message of the prophets. In Isaiah's day they said, 'Prophesy not to us what is right; speak to us smooth things, prophesy illusions, leave the way, turn aside from the path, let us hear no more of the Holy One of Israel' (Isaiah 30:10).

The prophet, however, had not only the task of bringing judgement to bear upon the life of the nation, and pointing out in forthright terms the dangers to it if the present policy and way of life were continued. He also had the task of declaring his unwavering faith in a better future, the day of the Lord, a time of justice and peace. The true prophet had both a lively awareness of the immediate and a visionary understanding of the distant future. His task was at one and the same time to pronounce judgement on the old order and to herald the new order. An incident in the life of Jeremiah epitomizes this dual role of the prophet.

In the last days of the old city of Jerusalem, Jeremiah lay in a dungeon cell within the city walls while the Chaldean armies laying siege to the city were encamped outside them. The army of Nebuchadnezzar had smashed its victorious way across Palestine, with nation after nation falling before it and suffering the scourge of pillage and plunder, of savagery and slavery, of destruction and despair. Only tiny Judah remained in defiance, but the beleaguered garrison could not hope to hold out much longer. Surrender daily became more inevitable. Jeremiah was in prison for his allegedly 'unpatriotic preaching'. His message was unpalatable to the nation's rulers as he had for a long time been foretelling the destruction of Jerusalem if the present policies of evil and corruption continued. Even in a dungeon cell he could not be silenced, for only the repentance of the people and a complete change in the national life could save the city, he declared.

One day Jeremiah received a visit in prison from his cousin Hanamel, asking him to buy a piece of land that had been in the family for generations. Jeremiah saw in this request a practical opportunity to demonstrate the word of the Lord to the nation. The request in itself was crazy. Who would buy land at such a time, when the whole countryside was overrun by the enemy? Nobody was buying or selling. But Jeremiah did just that.

He wrote out a bill of sale, signed it and had it solemnly witnessed. He weighed out the money and handed it to his cousin. The bill of sale he took and placed in an earthenware jar, sealing it and giving instructions that it was to be placed in safe keeping so that it could last for a long time. He looked forward to the day when 'houses and fields and vineyards shall again be bought in this land' (Jeremiah 32:15).

Jeremiah was staking his claim in the new society in the time of restoration, in the new creation that would follow the destruction of the old cities and the old way of life. The prophet did not withdraw his judgement upon the old regime. He clearly saw that it was doomed to destruction. Only one thing could alter that judgement and that was the repentance of the people and a basic change in the policy of the nation. Short of this he saw the end of Jerusalem as inevitable and the enslavement of her people as a terrible consequence of their disobedience to God and their refusal to hear the word of the Lord that had been proclaimed in their hearing.

Jeremiah proclaimed judgement upon the old order while declaring his faith in the new one: the new creation that would come about after the restoration. This new creation would be by the hand of God as surely as was the destruction of the old city. God was giving over into the hands of their enemies both the city he loved, and her people whom he counted as his own, because of their faithlessness and their refusal to hear his word.

If we turn now to the life of our own nation today we see a picture of economic and social confusion set against a backcloth of moral and spiritual decay. Few of our citizens can be unaware that we are living in days of enormous tension and social stress. This is due ostensibly to economic problems such as chronic inflation, with the incessant upward spiral of increasing prices and the demand for larger wages, salaries and profits. There are also the ever-growing tensions in industry between workers and management. There are the festering sores of racial conflict in our cities, where immigrants from the New Commonwealth have settled. There is the growing menace of the challenge to law and order upon our streets. There is the pollution of pornography in our newspaper shops, and the increasing boldness of the purveyors of vice and moral corruption in our society. There is the ever-increasing evidence of marriage and family breakdown, and all the consequent suffering, nervous strains and tensions inflicted upon the young and innocent as well as upon the guilty. And so we could go on, cataloguing the evidence of a sick society, but that is not the intention of this book. We have only to open our newspapers, buy a selection of glossy magazines, or watch TV for a few evenings to realize that there is something basically wrong with the national life of Britain.

The purpose of this book is not to amass evidence of a sick society. That is something any normally intelligent resident in this country could do in a few days. In any case that would be to examine the mere phenomenology of social sickness without identifying the real issues. Neither is it the task of this book merely to decry all the changes that have taken place in modern Britain over the past few generations. That would be to miss the immense benefits to mankind of many of the massive changes that have occurred, both through the development of science and technology and through changes in the social order.

The purpose of this book is to examine the 'signs of the times' and if possible to discern the *root causes* of the ailments in our national life. This is not a simple task in a highly complex urban industrial society. It does require some sociological skills and insights for the analysis of the trends, or 'processes', that are at work in our society today. Our objective is not, however, purely sociological. What we are undertaking is essentially a prophetic task. Whilst using all the sociological skills at our disposal, the analysis will be undertaken from a basically Biblical standpoint with the objective of discovering the word of God for our generation.

Prophecy is not the work of lengthy deliberation, although the prophet may mull over the word of the Lord for a long period before delivering it. It is the product of immediacy. It is given, not worked out. It is the result of God speaking to man and man listening and obeying. For a few brief moments time and eternity merge, the personality of God and the personality of man fuse, the vision of reality is communicated, the word of the Lord is given. It is, in its suddenness and vividness, like the rending of the heavens by lightning. It is, once it is given, irresistible and compelling in the urge to communicate.

That is how this book came to be written. The vision of reality was communicated by direct revelation from God. It was mulled over for a long time and studied in the context of sociological theory. Even then it was not written until the sign was given that the time was right. It has been written to enable Christians to understand what is happening in Britain today, to enable us to identify and grapple with the forces that are at work in our society. These forces are threatening to overwhelm and engulf us and to destroy the basis of Christian civilization.

The prophetic task laid upon the Church today is to be in vital communication with God through living under the authority of the Lordship of Jesus and being fully open to the power and direction of the Holy Spirit, while at the same time also being intimately aware of secular forces and understanding the socio-economic and political forces that are at work in our modern world. In this way Christians will be able to fulfil the prophetic task of the people of God at one of the great crisis points in history – to be able to understand the needs of man, to interpret the signs of the times and to bring the word of the Lord to our generation. If we succeed in this task the whole future history of mankind will be changed. If we fail – the consequences are unthinkable!

THEORETICAL
CONCEPTS

Where there is no one in authority the
people break loose.

Proverbs 29:18
(New English Bible)

CHAPTER TWO

THEORETICAL CONCEPTS

Introductory note

In chapters 3, 4 and 5 we shall be carrying out an analysis of the forces of change that are at work in Britain today. Our purpose is to try to understand what is happening in the life of the nation and to predict the likely outcome of the processes that are gathering momentum in our society. For the purpose of analysis we look separately at the Socio-Cultural Factors in chapter 3, the Political and Economic Factors in chapter 4, and the Spiritual Factors in chapter 5.

All these strands are closely interrelated and there is inevitably some overlap in treating the subject matter in this way. Strictly speaking religion is part of culture and is very difficult to treat in isolation from the moral concepts and total value system of a society. Nevertheless, I believe it is perfectly valid to separate the subject into the three areas we have delineated, because they represent three broad 'streams' or 'social forces' or 'developmental processes' that are having a profound effect upon the life of our nation today. They are moulding and reshaping the destiny of Britain in a manner that may well affect the future of the nation for generations to come.

It is therefore essential for there to be a widespread recognition of what is happening, of the trends, pressures and direction of the forces that are at work in Britain today.

In this chapter I have set out as simply as possible, for the non-professional reader, the theoretical basis (both socio-

logical and theological) of the analysis that is undertaken.
Where we are dealing with sociological concepts it is inevitable that the language of that subject be used and some
readers may find this unfamiliar. Those who do find it a
stumbling block, or who do not wish to grapple with the
theoretical concepts, may prefer to leave this chapter unread
and go on to chapter 3, where the analysis begins.

THEORIES OF SOCIAL CHANGE

Amongst the numerous theories of social change the three
outstanding systems of thought are:

(1) The Theory of Economic Determinism initially expounded by Karl Marx.
(2) The Functionalist Theory that originated with Bronis-
law Malinowski.
(3) The Social Action Theory of Talcott Parsons.

(1) *The Theory of Economic Determinism*

The main purpose of the Marxist theory of social change
was to provide a rationale for revolution. Through the theory
of dialectical materialism Marx worked out a rational and
scientific basis for rejecting industrial capitalism, and it was
only after he had developed the theory that he looked for
empirical evidence in the economic processes of capitalist
society to substantiate his views. Marx saw the main agent
of social change as being located in the economic foundation
of society. He believed that the type of economy determined
the culture, the values and even the belief system of the
society. Thus changes in the economic basis of a society are

primary, being causally determined by scientific laws. So economic changes trigger off changes in the superstructure of society whose real foundation is the economy. Marx's classic statement on the relationship between the foundational basis and the superstructure of society is, 'The totality of production relations constitutes the economic structure of society, the real basis upon which a legal and political superstructure arises and to which definitive forms of social consciousness correspond.

'The mode of production of the material means of life determines in general the social, political and intellectual processes of life.'[2]

The historical materialism of Marx asserts that all the ideas, the values, as well as the institutions, of a given social system are determined by the type of economy, and the social position of any individual within a given social system is determined by his relationship to the means of production. Thus Marx sees the whole of human history as being economically determined, and within modern industrial society the main agency of social change is the class struggle. It is the struggle between the 'haves' and the 'have nots', between those who have only their labour to sell and those who live by the exploitation of labour.

But this is not a conscious process in which individual actors are the deliberate agents of social innovation. Although Marx sees the agencies of change in terms of endogenous processes, the causal determinants themselves are exogenous.

Marx sees the whole cosmos as consisting in a system of interacting and ever changing parts, 'matter in motion', which is the real existential basis of human history and the precondition of social developmental processes. Nevertheless, he sees the contradiction or conflict between the forces of social production and social relationships as being the predicator of social change. While the struggle itself is inevitable, within the principle of determinism Marx nevertheless leaves

room for the individual partisan class fighter who understands the historical processes at work within society and
willingly places himself at a strategic point to participate
within them.

(2) Functionalist Theory

The theory of functionalism as developed by Malinowski is
based upon the conception of need. 'Need' in this case means
a set of conditions which are generated in the individual or
group within the context of culture. The most basic needs
are organic or biological – the need to get and to beget, the
need for food, shelter and the satisfaction of biological
impulses. Malinowski believes that any serious culture change
has to begin from the basic organic needs of man and then
proceed to the more complex related or secondary needs
which he groups under three headings – instrumental, recreative and integrative needs. The instrumental includes such
imperatives as economic, educational and political needs.
The integratives include knowledge, science and religion.
The recreative imperatives are art, music and games. These
are the economic, spiritual and social imperatives but the
significant factor is that Malinowski sees them as *imperatives*,
not as options which man can choose to ignore.

The theory of functionalism assumes that all social processes are causally determined. Malinowski saw man as being
liberated from the determinism of nature which binds all
other animals, but as being both the slave and the agent
of another determinism, that of culture. He saw culture itself
as being bound by yet another determinism, a system of
causally determined laws. Malinowski believed that culture
is a vast apparatus, partly physical, partly spiritual and partly
behavioural, which develops to meet the changing needs of
man in each generation and to enable him to cope with the
problems of living within a social and physical environment.

Culture thus is specifically functional: it equips the individual with the ability to live within a group situation, and enables the group to achieve social stability and to perform the activities necessary for survival. Any basic failure in the sequence of habitual activities, such as a failure to transmit the culture pattern to a new generation, would inevitably lead to the extinction of the whole cultural apparatus and with it the human group.

Malinowski[3] applies the Darwinian principle of natural selection, of 'survival of the fittest', to his social theory. He uses the concepts of evolution and diffusion and applies them to functionalism in order to understand the principles of social change. Through an evolutionary process cultural innovations are sifted through a sieve of selection. Only those that are the most fit to meet specific social needs survive to become part of the cultural apparatus. This applies in particular to the ideas, the religious beliefs and the values of society. Unless they are specifically related to meet the needs of man in a particular generation they will not survive. Through the concept of 'diffusion' Malinowski sees cultural interaction taking place whereby elements from different cultures are borrowed or transmitted from one another, thereby bringing about a process of cultural innovation.

There are thus two basic ways in which social change occurs. The first is where culture adapts to meet the changing needs of man in a changing natural order. The second is where a three-phase process of culture contact occurs. The first phase is where a situation of stable equilibrium exists, in which the customs, beliefs and institutions of a given society are relatively stable and passive. The second phase occurs with the introduction of an alien culture. The third phase takes the form of culture conflict, co-operation or compromise, as a result of which changes take place in both the indigenous and the intrusive cultures.[4]

(3) *The Social Action Theory*

The social action theory as developed by Parsons uses an analytical tool made up of four action systems which interpenetrate and interact with each other. These are: (1) Society, or the social system; (2) Man, or the personality system; (3) Culture, or the cultural system; (4) Nature, or the organic system. Parsons' starting point was the social system, which he defined as consisting in a 'plurality of interacting persons motivated in terms of a tendency towards the "optimization of gratification" and whose relation to their situations, including each other, is defined and mediated in terms of a system of culturally constructed symbols.'[5]

According to the action theory all social systems function in accordance with the four exigencies of goal seeking, adaptation, motivation and symbolization. Indeed the key problem in accounting for the functioning of social systems resolves itself around the question of the interactions and interrelationships of the adaptive, integrative, goal attainment and pattern maintenance subsystems. Thus it is inevitable that there will be a certain level of tension within every social system as a normal state of affairs. Without the existence of this tension there would be no change or growth possible within society, no adaptation, no innovation, no response due to new technology or the changing social or ecological milieu.

Social systems, like physical organisms, are constantly changing. The problems of social change arise when the equilibrium conditions under which the system normally functions are disturbed. In physical science equilibrium can be of three types: (a) stable, (b) partial and (c) unstable.

(a) In stable equilibrium the system, when disturbed, returns to its original condition.
(b) In partial equilibrium some units adjust, others do not.

(c) In unstable equilibrium the system continually re-adjusts so that the elements occupy new positions within a constantly changing equilibrium.

These rules need some modification when applying them to the processes of social change.

No social system remains unaltered indefinitely, nor when disturbed does it return unaltered to its original state. Thus the stable model of society is virtually unknown. The partial model has some basis in reality, but it is a well known sociological dictum that social change in any one institution results in change in other institutions. This is because of the complex interrelatedness of institutions within the social system. Unstable equilibrium is the normal case in society. Growth by differentiation and reduplication is a factor which acts constantly to disturb social equilibrium.

Growth entails changes and mutual adjustments in the elements of which the system is composed. Equilibrium and change are complementary processes. The equilibrium may be disturbed either by internal forces such as changes in the economy or in social legislation, or by external forces such as war or the impact of cultural influences from other social systems due, for example, to migration.

Summary

All three theories thus accept the principle of 'determinism' as underlying the social processes of change. They reduce the status of the individual social agent or innovator to a mere element in a predetermined system that obeys immutable scientific laws. Each of them, however, differs in its location of the primary sources of social change:

- For Marx this is located in the economy

- For Malinowski the crucial focus is human needs and their satisfaction. The cultural system adapts to vital needs by a process very similar to that of natural selection.
- Parsons believes that a system of role differentiation is the prime measure and manifestation of change. The process starts with the values underlying the system, and changes soon work through the whole functioning system.

Thus two outstanding facts are derived from these major sociological theories which are of immense significance for our present purpose.

(1) The first is that they all agree that man is driven by forces outside his own control. Man, both as an individual and mankind collectively, is seen to be at the mercy of social forces beyond his ability to control.

(2) The second is that there is no general agreement as to the primary source of the forces of social change that are at work in society, and that are basically affecting the lives both of individuals and of mankind.

It will be useful now if we spend a little time examining these two points which are important in formulating the crucial foci for our analysis.

(1) Determinism

All the major sociological schools of thought adopt a measure of determinism in relation to social change. The basic principles underlying the changes that take place in society are not controlled by the conscious decisions of individuals or even by the collective decisions of groups within a given society. The principles of social change are predetermined and are governed by factors in the order of creation, or the realm of natural phenomena, that obey causally determined laws in the same way as does the physical environment.

Most social theories see society as evolving through continuous processes of change and although there occur certain disturbances, in much the same way as mutations occur in physical science, the overall pattern continues to develop in accordance with known laws. These disturbances are due to the actions of individuals or groups in particular periods of history, but many social scientists would say that even these 'social mutations' are the predictable outcome of given sets of social conditions. Both Marxism and functionalism leave very little room for individual action. Man is seen as a product of the social environment. His values and beliefs are determined by the society in which he grows up and which inevitably predetermines the limits of his social actions. A child born into a peasant family in rural Pakistan will obviously have a very different cultural environment from a child born into a middle-class suburban Anglo-Saxon Protestant Christian family in England. They will differ in religion, language, customs and life-chances as fundamentally as if they came from different worlds.

Societies change through culture contact between one society and another as well as by internal interaction, but the processes of culture change are usually slow and are governed by laws in the same way as is the physical universe. The boundaries of social action, for societies as well as for man as an individual, are determined by the social conditions pertaining at any given point in time. Individual creativity and freedom of action are possible within certain limits, but the overall determining factors governing all social intercourse are as immutable as the laws operating in the physical universe.

Such a view of man as being subject to causally determined laws outside his own control does not in fact contrast at all sharply with a Biblical view of man. Paul, addressing the Athenian philosophers in the Areopagus (the forum at Mars Hill), stated his belief in one God, creator of all things, and then went on to declare, 'He created all the people of the world from one man, Adam, and scattered the nations across the face of the earth. He decided beforehand which should rise and fall, and when. He determined their boundaries' (Acts 17:26; The Living Bible).

Paul saw mankind as being driven by forces outside human control. He exhorted the Christians in Ephesus to find their 'strength in the Lord, in his mighty power' and to put on the whole armour which God provides. 'For our fight is not against human foes, but against cosmic powers, against the authorities and potentates of this dark world, against the superhuman forces of evil in the heavens' (Ephesians 6:12; New English Bible). Paul saw the whole of history as a cosmic battle between the forces of light and the forces of darkness. He believed the whole of creation was absorbed in this giant battle and that man, as part of the created order, was held in the vice-like grip of evil forces. These are the 'principalities and powers' (using the R.S.V. translation) of the unseen spiritual forces of evil that causally determine the behaviour of mankind.

Although Paul perceives the cosmic proportions of the conflict he is also well aware of the involvement of the individual in the battle. In Romans 7 he turns from the macro situation to the micro, and vividly portrays the helplessness of the individual caught up in the conflict and driven relentlessly towards destruction just as surely as the 'governing powers' of 'this passing age' are 'declining to their end' (1 Corinthians 2:6; N.E.B.). Societies are made up of individuals, and Paul recognizes that it is with man as an individual that the key to the solution, as well as the problem, must lie. Just as conflict in wider society is tearing the world of mankind apart and driving the nations towards inevitable destruction, so each individual is torn apart with internal conflict – all part of the battle between good and evil, light and darkness. But it is a battle that man cannot hope to win alone and unaided.

In order to identify and to try to understand what is happening within man, Paul personalizes the internal conflict to his own experience. He says, 'I do not understand my own actions. For I do not do what I want, but I do the very thing that I hate ... so then it is no longer I that do it, but sin which dwells within me.' Paul states that although he perceives with his rational mind what is good, yet he finds himself powerless to do good – and this despite the fact that he not only appreciates the good but wants to do it and wills himself to be good, his will is powerless against the forces of evil that are driving him. 'I can will what is right, but I cannot do it. For I do not do the good I want, but the evil I do not want is what I do' (Romans 7:15–19).

In describing this conflict Paul is putting into words the experience of every man who has reflected on his own behaviour. He states it in the form of a rule or law, 'I discover this principle, then: that when I want to do the right, only the wrong is within my reach. In my inmost self I delight in the law of God, but I perceive that there is in my bodily members a different law, fighting against the law that my reason approves and making me a prisoner under the law that is in my members, the law of sin' (Romans 7:21–23; N.E.B.). But Paul has not only wrestled with the problem, he has discovered the solution. He has realized that the forces of evil in the universe have become personalized within him so that he is enslaved. He is powerless to break away from their influence. He is driven by forces against which he cannot stand. He is like a man attempting to withstand the force of a hurricane. He is caught in open country as the wind gathers momentum across the land. He lies down flat on the ground in an attempt to reduce the wind resistance of

his body, but at its height the hurricane blows with such
force that it picks him up and hurls him to destruction.

Paul sees himself driven by powerful forces that will
eventually destroy him. Humanly speaking there is no
answer. He knows of no power great enough to withstand
the cosmic forces of evil that are let loose in the world and
that have become lodged in his body. 'What an unhappy
man I am! Who will rescue me from this body that is taking
me to death?' he cries. But the answer comes immediately,
it is there in his own vivid experience. 'Thanks be to God,
who does this through our Lord Jesus Christ!' (Romans 7/25;
Good News Bible).

The experience of being rescued from destruction, of
loosing the chains that shackled him to the spiritual forces
of evil that were overwhelming him, began, for Paul, on the
road to Damascus. It was here, in his first unforgettable
encounter with Christ, that Paul had his first taste of a new
power that spelt life as surely as the old powers of destruction
spelt death.

Marx also had an experience of life very similar to that
described by Paul in Romans 7. What he lacked was the
experience of the Damascus road. Indeed the experience of
powerlessness is one that is common to all mankind. This
is something not always appreciated by those who lack
positions of social status or wealth that apparently carry
great influence and power. Every social system, whether that
of a simple society, a complex democracy or a totalitarian
state, has its limitations and constraints which it places upon
each individual. Those who are on the lowest rung of the
social status ladder or at the bottom of the economic pile
look with envy at those in higher positions and imagine they
have great freedom and power to choose their actions. In
fact the reverse is often true. The greater the responsibility
carried, the greater the constraints and limitations placed
upon individual freedom of action. The more deeply we

reflect upon our social situation the more we recognize the limitations placed upon us and the power of the forces that are arrayed against us.[6]

Karl Marx's experience of alienation[7] in early childhood remained with him and coloured his thinking throughout his lifetime. Born into a Jewish family alienated from the local Jewish community in Trier as well as from provincial German society, he spent the last thirty-five years of his life in exile in England, living in a nation with which he never attempted to identify himself. Marx reflected his personal experience of alienation in his social and economic philosophy. He saw the whole history of the development of mankind as the history of man's alienation. Man was alienated from the world of Nature, from other men and from himself.

It was Hegel who first coined the concept of 'alienation' but Marx took it and developed it into a form of naïve idealism. He hated the typologizing of man in occupational categories such as farmer, fisherman, mechanic or writer. He wanted man to have the freedom to be a mechanic for part of the day and also to have time to fish and time to write. He believed that the prime source of alienation lay in the economic order that enslaved man and reduced him to a mere cog in the wheels of industry, a tool in the production process. In this part of his philosophy Marx is in line with the whole existentialist protest from Kierkegaard to Tillich which is a rebellion against the dehumanizing of man in industrial society. But Marx was not interested simply in improving the lot of the workers and still less in increasing their level of economic prosperity. He writes, 'An enforced increase in wages would be nothing better than a better remuneration of slaves and would not restore, either to the worker or to the work, their human significance and worth ... Even the equality of incomes which Proudhorn demands would only change the relation of the present day worker to his work into a relation of all men to work. Society would then be conceived as an abstract capitalist.'[8]

Marx believed that both the processes of production and the end product are sources of alienation. Through the process of work man is alienated from his own creative powers, his creativity becomes blunted and he becomes alienated from the world of natural phenomena. The product of the labour of his hands also becomes alien to man and eventually rules over him. He becomes alienated from his fellow men and even from himself. In worshipping the creation of his own hands man becomes a 'thing' – he is dehumanized. Instead of experiencing himself as a creative person he is in touch with himself only by the worship of the idol, he becomes estranged from his own life forces. This is the inevitable result of a society based upon individual private property in which man is deprived of the product of his own labours. In a capitalist system objects that man has produced become alien beings that dominate him. 'The labourer exists for the process of production and not the process of production for the labourer.' Thus the whole of man's relationships become affected. Human relationships become relationships between objects. This is because each man is alienated from the others and each of the others is alienated from human life.

Marx sees the forces of alienation at work in a capitalist society as being automatic and outside human control. They are determined by the economic order of society. The individual is powerless to resist their effect. Man is driven by forces beyond his control. He can only be liberated from the forces that destroy his humanity by a basic change in the economic order, that in turn will change the social order and set man free to be himself. It is self-realization with which Marx is ultimately concerned and which he sees as the result of socialism. The liberation of man from the destroying forces of alienation can only be accomplished by the workers acting together as a universal class, in the interests of humanity as a whole, and creating a socialist society.

Thus while both Paul and Marx agree that man is driven by forces of destruction that are outside his control, they come to very different solutions to the problem. Paul believes that man is unable to liberate himself, while Marx believes that man acting collectively can create the conditions that set him free. Both Paul and Marx offer hope to man locked in the shackles of slavery, but each has an opposite starting point. Paul looks to the ultimate transformation of society through the immediate transformation of the individual. Marx looks to the ultimate liberation of the individual through the primary transformation of society. But the most radical difference between Marx and Paul lies in the nature of the hope they offer. Paul offers a hope based upon the certainty of personal experience whereas Marx offers a hope based upon a theory of change – a conceptual philosophical construction.

The hope of liberation for Paul is not a vague theory but a practical reality. He has already experienced the victory and is living the new life and enjoying the new relationships that follow the breaking of the chains of slavery. He can speak with the certainty and conviction of personal experience. Christ has set him free: whereas once he was blind now he can see, whereas once he was dead now he is alive. Whereas once he was alienated from God and from his fellow man now he is a son of God. Christ has 'broken down the dividing wall of hostility'. He is able to call God 'Abba, Father', and to enter into relationships of brotherly love with other men, regardless of social rank, even with slaves (e.g. Onesimus). Hence the certainty of the hope for Paul lies in the realization of the hope through the experience of being 'in Christ'.

Perhaps the failure of Marxism lies in its realization in the U.S.S.R. Man has not been liberated from the forces of oppression by a change in the economic order generated by a social revolution. The hope of freedom is still a hopeless ideal when the forces that generate exploitation and oppression are still untamed and active in the world. It is here that we reach the real nub of the problem and we must ask ourselves the question: what is the fundamental source of the forces that are driving mankind to destruction?

(2) Source of Social Change

(a) Point of Intervention

The second major question facing us is, what is the primary source of the forces that are driving mankind? From where do the forces emanate that are gathering momentum and sweeping through our society? A great deal hangs on the answer to this question because it indicates to us the right point at which an intervention could effectively be made that would change the course and direction of the forces now at work in our society. If we intervene at the wrong point we shall not be able to halt the forces of social change that are already in motion, and we shall simply generate a lot of frustration.

There is today a lot of well-meaning but ill-informed activity amongst Christians, social reformers and others who are concerned about the state of our nation. They propose a great variety of measures intended to deal with the situation, chiefly repressive measures, aimed at the normative structure of society. These usually include such proposals as bringing back capital punishment and stiffer gaol sentences or other punitive measures as a deterrent to crime, and many other proposals intended to deal with the problems of law and order in our society. But what is the point of attempting to deal with the problems of law and order if these are the mere *symptoms* of an underlying problem? It is like someone having sores on his body and simply treating them with ointment instead of dealing with the blood disorder which is their real root cause.

Similarly in society we have to diagnose and treat the *source* of the social problems rather than simply be concerned with the problems themselves. We are too often concerned with the mere phenomenology of social ailments rather than with the ailments themselves and their root causes. We can waste so much energy in rushing around attempting this solution and that, passing social legislation or making organizational changes in society that have little or no effect on the general standards of life. It is like knocking down old decaying, rotting slum properties, building huge new tenement blocks of rented flats and rehousing the former slum dwellers. If we do nothing to change their social values and attitudes, within a very few years the new housing accommodation will also be reduced to a slum and the people will be just as critical of their new accommodation as they were of the old. This has happened time after time in our inner-city areas. Within a year or two brand new housing developments have been turned into the foulest slums, and vast sums of money are required annually for maintenance of whole areas that are regarded as social disasters.

There are numerous other examples of social intervention at the wrong point, in a vain attempt to halt processes of change that are driving society towards a point of disorientation. Inevitably they are fruitless and lead either to frustration or to disaster. Patching up the breaches in the social system is a useless exercise. It is like children playing sand-castles on the beach with the incoming tide. The first waves lap gently around the outer defences of the castle. Then each wave grows bolder and stronger until the full attack of the relentless tide is mounted. As breaches appear in the wall on one side the children patch them up with wet sand, but by this time another wave has broken down the wall on the other side. The moment that is repaired there is another breach until finally a great wave washes right over the entire outer wall and it is not long before the inner defences fall anu the whole sand-castle sinks gently into the sea – turrets, keep, towers and walls, all gone without trace.

(b) Value Theory

Our concern is to delineate the primary sources of social change that generate the forces at work in our society. It is here that Parsons' Value Theory of social organization has more to offer than other sociological schools of thought. Parsons uses a system functions analytical tool. He sees the totality of human life, or 'action frame of reference', as being divided into four levels of systems. These are (1) the cultural, (2) the social, (3) the personality and (4) the organistic. These are not higher and lower levels of human activity, although sometimes Parsons appears to refer to them as such. They are, for analytical purposes, seen to be distinct systems, but 'open' rather than 'closed' and therefore having a high level of interpenetration and interaction between them. Parsons distinguishes each of these systems on the basis of the major type of function each performs within the totality of human life.[9]

Cultural systems perform the function of pattern maintenance, i.e. maintaining the major values of human existence. Social systems have their main focus upon integration, or creating order in social life. Personality systems are primarily concerned with the function of goal attainment, or achieving goals in the social environment. Organistic systems deal largely with the function of adaptation, or adapting human life to the natural world.

Parsons believes that below the organistic systems there lies the natural environment which provides from the natural environment the prime source of energy, or resources, which feeds into the whole of human life. Above the cultural systems lies the realm of 'ultimate reality' which influences the values upon which the whole of human life is based.

Parsons uses the same scheme of system functions analysis for each of the major component parts of the total system. An action system where we are dealing with the social system, the cultural system, the personality system or the organistic, demands an adaptive subsystem, a goal gratification subsystem, a pattern maintenance subsystem and an integrative subsystem.

If we look at the social system by way of example we see that:

(1) Society must provide for the utilization of available resources which means that the society must be adaptive. In the adaptive subsystem of the social system we are dealing with institutions such as the economy through which action organisms obtain necessary resources from the natural environment.

(2) Secondly, both individuals and groups in society must be able to recognize certain ends and needs as being desirable for the maintenance of individual and group life, and on such a basis be able to organize life towards goal attainment.

(3) Thirdly, society must be preserved from disintegration by disruptive forces of change. Thus the specific patterns of activities, beliefs and values of society must be guarded from violent and destructive change. Hence the pattern maintenance subsystem which is composed of such institutions as religion, education, and the family, is concerned with preserving and perpetuating the basic values of the total social system which are derived from the overriding cultural system.

(4) Fourthly, society is continually changing, which is, of course, the property of all living organisms, and therefore the different social units within the total system must continually adjust to each other so as to maximize their

effective functioning within the total system. The integrative subsystem which focuses around the 'societal community' or 'patterned normative order' allows the necessary internal adjustments and adaptation to take place.[10]

Parsons' concept of Value Theory assumes a set of common values contained within the cultural system that contribute towards the overall unity of all social systems. The dominant values are those held in common by most or all of the members in a given society, although their basic meanings are determined by perceptions derived from ultimate reality. These values may change over a period of time, primarily as a result of changing perceptions of ultimate reality, but these alterations are normally so slow that the values themselves may be considered to be constant.

The values of a society serve to legitimize the whole normative structure. They legitimize the norms that control the activities of society and individuals within each subsystem, through the process of institutionalization. Individuals as well as social groups are guided by the values of society and controlled by its norms that have become internalized within individual personalities through socialization. To the degree that individuals act upon the internalized norms, they reinforce those norms within the social system and affirm the values of the society that are the foundation of that system.

The common or shared values of a society that are drawn from the cultural system, shape and control all social life as they are expressed through the norms which are institutionalized within individual members of that society. According to Parsons 'that a system of value-orientations held in common by the members of a social system can serve as the main point of reference for analysing structure and process in the social system itself may be regarded as a major tenet of modern sociological theory'.[11]

Parsons has been criticized by those who do not like him postulating the existence of a realm of 'ultimate reality', but Parsons does not state that all values derive directly from ultimate reality, he says that the realm of ultimate reality gives 'meaning and objectivity' to values. Parsons has also been criticized on the grounds that his whole elaborate complex of ideas is not a theory at all but a set of analytical concepts. This is not the place to enter into the ongoing sociological debate, but we simply should note that Parsons, like all other sociologists, has his critics. There is no such thing as an authoritative body of sociological theory universally acceptable. We have adopted Parsons' Value Theory as being amongst the most academically respectable of modern sociological theories. It seems to provide us with a more satisfactory base for answering the fundamental problems of the source of social change than most sociological schools of thought.

According to Parsons the crucial focus in the process of social change lies not in the economy, as Marx believed, but in the value system. Changes in the value system have what Parsons calls a 'high impact' on all the other elements in the social system. While he does not see changes in the value system as being the *only* source of social innovation, he allocates to the value system the highest level of impact in terms of its effect upon the entire social system and the production of creative social change.[12]

(c) The Protestant Ethnic

Changes in the value system rapidly affect norms and work back to affect the entire substructure of the system. In modern history the most outstanding example of the way in which fundamental social changes have been initiated by a change in the value system may be seen in the Reformation. The teachings of Luther and Calvin, together with the ascetic ideals of monasticism, gave rise, through a process of secularization, to the Puritan ethic, or what is more popularly known as the 'Protestant Ethic'. This in turn created the ideological climate that fostered the growth of capitalism. The significance of Puritanism in the Industrial Revolution lay in the fact that it had already appeared in precisely those areas and in the specific groups which later became involved in initiating industrialization. As Max Weber pointed out, the Protestant Ethic legitimized not only profit making but also the instrumental use of human beings. Thus the *value system* of the older community was overthrown before the economic, technological, political and social revolutions associated with the factory system were completed. Religious change therefore anticipated, and provided the necessary ideological prerequisite for, the social change that facilitated the progress of the Industrial Revolution in England.

Weber nowhere claimed that the Protestant Ethic was the *cause* of the rise of capitalism, but his essay 'The Protestant Ethic and the Spirit of Capitalism' argued that the Protestant Reformation *created the ideological climate* that fostered the growth of capitalism.[13] Weber's essay has been the subject of more debate, elaboration and controversy than any other sociological writing since its publication in 1920. Despite the enormous interest generated by this short essay, and the vast amount that has been written on the subject, Weber's central theme has withstood the test of the severest examination. Apart from Robertson in the 1920s,[14] Fanfani in the '30s,[15] and Samuelson in the '50s,[16] few sociologists have denied its validity.

Weber established a clear link between Protestantism as it developed from the teachings of Luther and Calvin and the rise of capitalism. The evidence produced from numerous research projects has confirmed this continuing link. In countries where Protestants and Catholics live intermingled, the Protestants invariably occupy prominent positions in business disproportionate to their numbers. In France, for example, the influence of the Protestants in business is astonishing in view of their small numbers. The objection that their minority status stimulates their economic activity is countered by the data from a country like Germany where there is a more or less evenly balanced population. This evidence is examined by Andreski in an essay on Catholicism and Protestantism.

Andreski notes that Protestantism, especially Calvinism, taught thrift, but that thrift alone is not enough. 'An economic system whose propelling force is private accumulation of capital will not develop very fast if people are inclined to stop working as soon as they reach a certain level of affluence. Progress of such a system requires that those who have already enough for their needs should go on working and accumulating. The connection with Protestantism, particularly in its Calvinist variety, is that it taught people to work as a form of prayer, and the growth of possessions as the evidence of a state of grace. Another important influence of Protestantism was its insistence on work as the only legitimate road to riches. Other religions, of course, also prohibit robbery and theft, but Protestant puritanism is unique in condemning gambling. The religious ideals of work, thrift and enrichment without enjoyment and by means of work only, constitute what Weber calls "worldly asceticism". It is extremely plausible that a creed which preached such asceticism did in fact stimulate the growth of capitalism.'[17]

We must beware, however, of assuming that Protestantism only had an effect upon the economic activities and institutions of society. As Eisenstadt points out, 'the transformative effects of Protestantism were not limited only to the central institutions and symbols of society but also to other aspects of the institutional structure of modern societies, and especially to the development of new types of roles, role structure and role sets and to motivations to undertake and perform such roles. The essential core of Weber's Protestant Ethic thesis, as distinct from Weber's wider discussions of the transformative effects of Protestantism, focuses on one aspect of this problem – the development of the role of the economic entrepreneur and of the specific setting within which this role could become institutionalized.'[18]

Eisenstadt argues that Protestantism not only affected the economic institutions of Western society but had a fundamentally creative effect upon every aspect of life. It not only redefined roles and goals, but as these became institutionalized within society the effect was to produce new structural organizational patterns. Protestantism played a crucial creative role in society not only by reshaping its structure but also by providing the motivation for change. It did this by initiating new social goals and providing the spiritual/ethical motivation towards their attainment, and the drive behind individual identification with the new goals.

Eisenstadt summarizes: 'Thus we see that the transformative potential of Protestantism could affect the development of new roles in three different directions: first, in the definitions of specific new roles with new types of goals, defined in autonomous terms and not tied to existing frameworks; second, in the development of broader institutional, organizational and legal normative settings which could both legitimize such new roles and provide them with necessary resources and frameworks to facilitate their continuous working; and last, in the development of new types of motivation, of motivations for the understanding of such roles and for identifying with them.'[19]

Summary

We have seen that the major sociological theories of change take a basically determinist standpoint. A Biblical view of the nature of man and society is not fundamentally opposed to such a view. On the contrary, Biblical evidence, from the early Hebrew writings through to the New Testament, including the witness of the great eighth-century BC prophets, all agrees that if man is not *led* by the Spirit of God he will be *driven* by the forces of evil that are let loose in our world.

There is, however, no general agreement among sociologists as to the *source* of the forces that are driving mankind. Parsons takes the view that the major source of social change lies in the value system underlying the total social system, and he further posits the existence of a realm of ultimate reality from which the values of society are drawn or derive meaning and substance. Christians go further than this and link the realm of ultimate reality with the presence and being of God, from whom emanate all ultimate values. Whether or not Christians are right in looking to God as the source of all ultimate values it is not the purpose of this book to argue. We simply take note of the fact. What is of relevance for our present task is that we have established that academically it is perfectly sound to argue in terms of sociological theory that the primary source of social change lies not in the economy, or in the family, or in law and government, or in any other social institution, but in the value system of a society. Thus in order to effect basic changes in the structures of a society we have to change the values of that society.

This is a point of fundamental significance for Christians because it means that our total strategy of evangelism and witness should be geared towards changing the values of society. It means, moreover, that programmes of social reform, even if inspired by Christian precepts, unless closely linked with a value orientation and part of a strategy of value change, are a waste of time and energy. At best they are no more than social first aid. At worst they can act as a drug to delude men that they are 'improving' society and that they only have to make a little more effort to reach a kind of earthly Utopia or to create a kingdom of heaven upon earth.

Without a basic change in the values of the individual a man is still a helpless victim of forces beyond his personal ability to control. Similarly without a basic change in the values of society, mankind collectively is powerless to stand against the forces that are driving him towards destruction. This is both sociologically and theologically sound and is the theoretical concept underlying the thesis of this book

SOCIO-CULTURAL FACTORS

Where there is ignorance of God, the people run wild
Proverbs 29:18
(The Living Bible)

CHAPTER THREE

SOCIO-CULTURAL FACTORS

Phenomenology of Change

It is obvious even to the least observant student of history that the twentieth century has been the greatest period of change since the beginning of mankind. For our present task it is important to try to see why such radical and far reaching changes should be concentrated into such a comparatively short period of time. We also want to identify the processes at work within society that promote change, and to wrestle with the problems of trying to trace the sources of the forces that underlie the processes. Our purpose is to try to understand what is happening in the life of our nation and to predict the likely outcome of the developmental processes that are shaping and reshaping the life of the nation. It is not our intention to spend too much time in looking in any detail at the changes that have taken place in twentieth-century Britain, but it is relevant to note them in a short synoptical survey as the backcloth to our discussion.

We shall therefore take a brief look at these changes under three headings: (1) Technology, (2) Demography, (3) Culture.

(1) Technology

The technological advances that have been made during the twentieth century have been so immense that they almost read like a science fiction story. Within the lifetime of many people still living we have gone from the age of steam power to the age of nuclear power, from the early motor car with its simple internal combustion engine to space exploration with highly complex giant interplanetary rockets, from the rifle to the hydrogen bomb, from the adding machine to the computer, from the gas lamp to neon lights, from the telegraph to colour television. Within a single lifetime there has been a technological revolution of mind-boggling proportions. It is not an exaggeration to say that the senior citizens of today have seen the face of the earth changed by man's inventive genius and his ruthless exploitation of natural resources. They have seen the waters fouled, the atmosphere polluted, vast industrial complexes constructed, great cities and conurbations arising to swallow seventy-six per cent of our country's entire population and creating basic changes in the life style and culture of countless millions of people.

Of course, all the technological changes have not been bad, they have brought untold benefits to mankind in a multitude of ways. The advance of medical science has resulted in spectacular improvements in the health of the nation and has doubled the life expectation of the working classes in less than a century. Technology in the home, especially in the kitchen, has taken the drudgery out of life for the housewife and opened up for her a whole new range of life chances. The changes in the methods of production have virtually abolished sweated labour. No doubt before the end of this century there will be further spectacular advances in automation with the gradual introduction of silicon chips.

(2) Demography

The process of urbanization that is the twin counterpart of industrialization has continued to depopulate the countryside and to create the twentieth-century phenomenon of the overspill town and the vast ever expanding conurbations that fill the land with concrete. Urban and suburban living have changed the basic way of life for millions within a single lifetime. New forms of human relationships are demanded when we live in close proximity with strangers and those not of our own kith and kin or even of our own race and nation. New and complex forms of social organization are needed. In a single lifetime there have been far reaching changes in the whole structure of society which have affected in some way every part of life for every individual in Britain. Social class distinctions have become blurred by the high rate of social mobility. Education has opened up the professions to people of all social-class backgrounds, while the massive strides taken towards complete equality of the sexes have eradicated the discrimination of centuries and brought about radical and fundamental changes in the social order.

Speed and ease of travel have resulted in a great deal of population movement, not only within Britain from country-side to town and from city to city, but also in the high rate of emigration and immigration. The past twenty-five years have seen an unprecedented outward flow of British citizens to all parts of the world, especially to the Old Commonwealth and the U.S.A. This has been more than matched by the two million immigrants from the New Commonwealth who have come to settle in Britain. The vast majority of them have made their homes in the great industrial urban complexes of the Midlands and the South East, including the London area. They have brought with them new cultures, new social values, customs, and religions that have produced a multi-cultural, multi-racial, multi-religious population that was hitherto entirely unknown in this country. A pluralistic society inevitably produces conflict, especially in the early years, between people of vastly different backgrounds who had previously no knowledge of each other or of their respective traditions. Tensions are inevitable, but they are compounded when the new-comers are of a different race, culture, religion and nationality! They are further intensified when the immigrants themselves move into an area which already suffers from social stress because of lack of social amenities or shortage of basic facilities, or rising unemployment. If all three of these factors occur at the same time in the same place, as is the situation in some areas of Britain, the conflict is inevitably intensified.

(3) Culture

The rise of the pop culture in the mid-1950s is generally regarded as the beginning of the social revolution that has been shaking Britain to its foundations during the past twenty-five years. The pop culture began in what appeared to be a harmless, but unusually exuberant, youthful challenge to adult society. It was heralded by Bill Haley's film *Rock Around the Clock* which had already taken America by storm, and when it was shown in British cinemas the teenagers began ripping up seats, and dancing in the aisles, shouting and chanting and producing scenes of wild ecstasy hitherto unknown in these islands. Exaggerated press reports led to a heightened atmosphere of expectation at every showing of the film and produced a bandwagon effect.

Although but a small event in itself, this film heralded the beginnings of the teenage mania for music that is especially related to their own age group. For any new social movement to catch on it has to have a culture of its own. Young people found this in music of a particular type which gave them an identity and a peer group distinctiveness. This in turn quickly led to distinctive fashions in clothing for young people, hair styles, and even language. The youth revolution was on. It occurred at a time when young people were beginning to earn proportionately higher wages relative to the adult population than at any time in the history of Britain. Britain was enjoying her share of the industrial boom of the post Second World War reconstruction period.

Young people in the mid-1950s had greater spending power than ever before. This was a new social phenomenon and here was a social group ripe for exploitation in a capitalist society. Here was a group of consumers with considerable purchasing power and very few responsibilities, hence they represented a new and untapped market. Manufacturers soon began to compete in the new market and to produce a range of goods especially geared to the needs and tastes and fashions of teenagers. Records, record players, hi-fi equipment, musical instruments as well as clothing and a wide range of other consumer articles, all became geared to the new customers. Gradually the teenage market became more and more lucrative and dominant in the commercial world.

With such a basic economic shift in purchasing power and marketing directions it was inevitable that significant changes in the social order should follow. The cult of youth began. Young people began to enjoy a prominence never before accorded to them in an age-dominated society. Soon even the position of children within the family and in wider society was to be affected. The Victorian child who was seen and not heard, and who was spoilt if the rod was spared, disappeared from the life of the nation. Family life was affected. The adolescent challenge to the authority of the parents spread to the children who no longer automatically obeyed the voice of their elders. Education was affected. Strict discipline in the classroom disappeared. A new breed of teachers was coming out of the colleges of education in the '50s, who were applying new techniques of learning whereby the child and the teacher participated in a partnership of discovery that was a new dimension in education. Children were encouraged to think for themselves, to undertake projects, to enter fully into the discovery method of learning rather than the old one-way communication of 'talk and chalk' whereby they sat passively at their desks and listened to the teacher. They were no longer punished for not learning, they were encouraged to be creative and they were taught to be persons in their own right.

The change in the attitudes towards authority amongst schoolchildren and adolescents brought about radical changes within the family, at the same time as other social pressures were also weakening family ties. Despite the advent of television in almost every home the family was becoming less home-centred. Leisure activities began to be sought more and more outside the home. Marriage breakdown became more common and was eventually recognized by changes in the law to facilitate easier divorce.

Social values have undergone rapid and radical changes throughout the last twenty-five years. Changes in moral values have been reflected in changes in the law, which in turn have had the effect of further liberalizing moral attitudes. The relaxation of the laws on censorship has resulted not simply in the rise of the pornographic industry but in the free availability of 'soft porn' on the ordinary newspaper stands, while blue cinema clubs and the showing of X certificate films have become commonplace in every major city. Changes in public attitudes towards moral values have also been effected by the mass media and the relaxation of censorship upon newspapers and television.

The rise of radicalism in many different forms has been a feature of the past twenty-five years. The popularity of the 'New Left', and radical attitudes towards 'the Establishment' and traditionalism in every form, have been linked with the pop culture and the revolt of young people against all the traditional values of society. It has been an age marked by protest movements. The Campaign for Nuclear Disarmament in the 1950s was the forerunner of many politically orientated social protest movements. Movements connected with race and the protest against racism have been almost too numerous to mention. The women's lib movement that has successfully brought about changes in the law, making discrimination on the grounds of sex illegal, has been amongst the more successful campaigns. Some of these movements have had their counterparts campaigning for the opposite values. This has been notable particularly in the fields of race relations and abortion. The pro-abortion lobby of the 1960s succeeded in making it possible for abortions to be obtained on the National Health Service. This was followed by the anti-abortion lobby of the 1970s, campaigning on such slogans as 'The Right to Live' and building up public opinion against easy abortion. All these movements have had their effect upon social values, and have produced a period of radical change in the culture of the nation at a time when there has been a notable lack of authoritative yardsticks or basic principles to guide the formation of ethical standards. Traditionally these standards have been drawn from religion, but religion itself has been changing throughout the period since the end of the Second World War. The past twenty-five years have seen a remarkable decline in the social significance of Christianity as the national religion. The practice of church-going has declined to around ten per cent of the nation. The loss of significance of Christianity in Britain has occurred at a time of anti-Establishment attitudes amongst the young that further exacerbate the gap between the institutional churches and the ordinary non-church-going masses. It has coincided also with the rise of a form of neo-paganism closely linked with materialism.

The rise in the general standard of living, the increase in the general level of wages, plus the boom in consumer goods and the advertising on the mass media of every kind of consumer product have further undermined religious beliefs. The gods of a materialistic society are closely linked with its social values, its material aspirations and acquisitiveness. In Britain the neo-paganism has coincided with the rise of religious pluralism due largely to the impact of immigration.

The introduction of Eastern religions to Britain has resulted in the growing popularity of mystery religions and different types of polytheism. It has also been closely linked with an increasing interest in the occult and the growth of various forms of spiritism. Numerous cults have arisen during the past twenty-five years that have attracted a lot of publicity and have been particularly attractive to young people searching for an identity in an age of mass production and excessive bureaucratization.

The rise of religious pluralism and the loss of significance of Christianity as the traditional religion of the nation have had a major effect upon changing the culture of the national life. It has occurred at a time when social values are being challenged with unprecedented force and when every aspect of personal and social life has been changing due to basic changes in the economy and the demographic structure of society. Thus the challenge to the authority of traditional values has occurred at a time when the foundations of the nation's belief system were being eroded at an unprecedented pace. The two have inevitably interacted and produced a period of massive culture change such as has never before been known in Britain. We shall return to this theme again when we look at the institutional structure of society and the way in which this is affected by the processes of social change.

Processes of Social Change

We need now to take a brief look at the processes of social change and the way in which they work in our society. Change occurs through the operation of social processes and as we have seen in chapter 2, there is no one authoritative theoretical system to account for the way in which the whole phenomenon of change takes place. It is sometimes argued that to attempt to separate social processes from social structure leads to false analysis. It is argued that what we are looking at is not two distinct types of phenomena but the same phenomenon examined from two different standpoints. In other words, the working out of social processes leads to social structures, and social structures are comprised of the tangible evidence of social processes viewed at one point in time.

Thus the major variable separating structure from process is time. The question then arises, 'Do we look at social phenomena as they change and develop over a period of time, or as they appear at one point in time?' One of the limitations of the structural functionalist analysis is its preoccupation with social structure. Structural analysis can easily lend itself to over-simplification due to the concentration on average or typical situations. The structural functionalists tend to be primarily concerned with the dominant, legitimized, institutionalized structures at a particular point in time, rather than with seeing them as part of a developmental process that is continually ongoing.

Perhaps an even greater limitation of the structural functionalist approach is its tendency to be so concerned with the dominant majority in a society as to overlook the deviant minorities who often play the most significant social role in terms of initiating creative social change. It is usually the effect of the minorities upon social values that initiates change in the normative structure of society. Yet it is here that the structural functionalists themselves recognize the primary source of social change. Hence our concern is with the right evaluation of social processes and social structures. In a brief analysis such as we are able to undertake in this chapter, we can do no more than refer the reader to the continuing debate in sociology and indicate the main direction of the theoretical approach that we are taking.

The three social theories outlined in chapter 2 all recognize the possibility of change taking place due to movement *within* the social system. In Marxism the endogenous

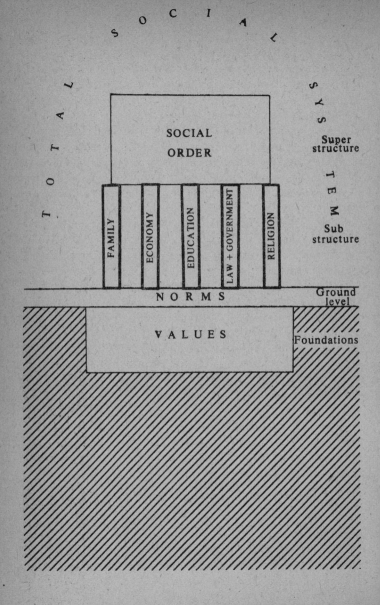

processes are considered to be the normal means of effecting change. Marx basically accepted an evolutionary view of the maturation of social processes within the system until they reached the point where the ground was sufficiently prepared for revolution.

At that point the slow natural evolutionary transformation process would give birth to the new social order as part of the ongoing process of dialectical change. Malinowski also recognized the slow process of evolutionary change but saw this as part of the response of the social order to the changing needs of man. Thus evolutionary change was interpreted in a functionalist framework. Parsons saw change within the system as stemming from charismatic innovation such as that of the religious or political leader who denounced the old way and pointed to a new way. Thus Parsons saw the primary source of social change as arising from the normative system and effecting consequential changes in the social order.

It is a useful model for the purpose of analysis if we regard the total system in the form of a building. Below ground we have the foundations and above ground we have the structure of the building. The building above ground is divided into two sections, with a substructure consisting of reinforced concrete pillars which raise the whole building high above ground level, and then the superstructure is built on top of the pillars.

In this figure of the total social system, the foundation consists of the normative structure, that is, the values, ideas and norms of the society. The substructure consists of the five major social institutions, namely:

The Family
The Economy
Education
Law and Government
Religion

The superstructure consists of the multitudinous social institutions, such as the welfare and health services, voluntary associations, leisure pursuits, the entertainment world and the whole proliferation of social organization.

Let us now examine the way in which change affects the total social system. It is a basic sociological dictum that:

> *where one of the five major social institutions experiences a radical change all the others are automatically affected.*

This may be illustrated from the life of a single individual as well as from society as a whole. For example, a man employed in the aircraft industry may lose his job due to an economic recession in the industry. This recession may be due to the political action of central government in ordering a cutback in defence spending. This political action may have been brought about by the agitation of a minority pressure group urging pacifist policies, due to their religious belief. The man's loss of his job may cause stress within the family that leads to marriage breakdown and the splitting of the family. Thus four major social institutions – the family, the economy, the political system and religion – all played a part in this particular drama. A change in one brought about changes in the others, but which was the primary source of change? At first glance it would appear that the family broke down due to the man losing his job, in other words the family was affected by the economy. But on closer examination it is clear that the job redundancy was caused by political action due in turn to religiously motivated pressures. Thus religion was the primary source of innovation that caused the chain reaction eventually ending in the break-up of the family. The interesting thing to note about this little illustration is that it was not religion as an institution, but a religious ideology or value that became institutionalized within a pressure group that was the actual primary source of creative innovation.

If we now turn from our micro situation to the total social system we see that the same chain effect of interaction between the major institutions occurs as a regular social phenomenon. A major change in the economy will soon affect the family. For example, the basic changes in the means of production introduced during the Industrial Revolution brought about fundamental changes in the family life of the nation. The hand looms and cottage industries disappeared, being replaced by the factory and the machine. Families had to leave the countryside and find new homes in the rising urban complexes, and members of the family had to learn new occupations and skills to earn a living in an industrial economy. Fundamental changes in the structure and function of the family were brought about. Whereas previously the family had a common purse and a common economic pursuit, now each member was paid an individual wage and each one worked in a different occupation, probably in a different factory. Thus the simple solidarity of the agrarian peasant family was broken down and the way was opened up towards the individuation of a complex urban industrial society.

Urban living demanded new forms of social organization and this in turn imposed further changes upon the structure and function of the family. For example, the pre-industrial family was responsible for the socialization of the young and the care of its own elderly, sick and handicapped members. Gradually all of these functions have been eroded. The formal socialization of the young has now been very largely delegated to the schools, whilst the care of the elderly, sick and handicapped has increasingly become the responsibility of state institutions. New forms of social organizations in urban industrialized society have necessitated new social regulations and have led to our modern highly complex legal and political law enforcement system. Even religion in Britain has undergone basic changes due to industrialization. Religion was one of the major integrative forces contributing to the solidarity of the pre-industrial agrarian family, with its simple basis of faith and shared belief system that closely linked rural man with the world of nature from which he derived his being and his sustenance. Urban industrial man, living in a world of concrete, alienated from nature, exposed to pluralism and secularism developed new expectations and requirements of religion and forms of institutionalized religion.

Thus all the major social institutions were affected by the Industrial Revolution, in a chain sequence beginning with basic changes in the economy that eventually permeated through to effect basic changes in every part of the social system. Similarly we could illustrate the same principle of chain reaction occurring resulting from a change in any one of the major social institutions. For example, if there were a radical change in the political system to that of the totalitarian state this would affect the economy and the structure and function of the family. It would also undoubtedly effect basic changes in the educational system and would no doubt impose restrictions on the belief system that would eventually produce changes in the whole institution of religion.

If we took religion as our starting point we could, in the same way, demonstrate that radical changes would take place throughout all the other social institutions affecting the entire social system. An illustration of this may be found in the Wesleyan Methodist Revival of the eighteenth century at a time when England was on the verge of social revolution. Most historians agree that the preaching of the Wesleys had a powerful effect upon the working classes that not only effected basic changes in ethical standards, personal morality and in family organization, but also proved a major factor in steering the nation away from civil war. Thus, due to the close interaction between all the component parts of the total social system, any basic change in one of the major social institutions produces an immediate effect upon all other parts of the system. We may add a further dictum in terms of the forces of social change:

> *the more rapid and the more radical the change in any one part of the system, the more quickly will the effect spread to other parts of the system and the more fundamental will be the changes transmitted.*

The situation we have now reached in modern Britain is that during the past twenty-five years since the advent of the pop culture, all parts of the social system have been experiencing varying degrees of change. Change during this period has not simply been confined to the social system but has also been experienced within the cultural system as well. We shall return to this point again shortly. For the moment our prime concern is with the social system, where each of the major social institutions has been undergoing radical and fundamental changes. These changes have worked backwards to affect the underlying norms beneath each institution, and have gone still further down to reach the values underlying the norms. There has also been an upward effect, partly due to feedback and partly to a *sui generis* movement.

If we take education as an example there have been basic changes in the *philosophy* of education. Thus the value underlying the normative structure of the basis of the institution has undergone a change which has sped upwards through the system. The old philosophy of education which saw education primarily as a learning exercise, exam-orientated, changed to give a broader view of education as contributing basically to the process of self-maturation. This change of value sped upwards through the system to change the institutional nature of the school and its organization and function, including the relationships between staff and pupils, and the exercise of discipline, punishment and rewards. There have been many experimental changes in teaching methods, such as thematic teaching rather than subject teaching, and in the assessment of results and attainment, such as 'continuous assessment' rather than terminal examinations. The organizational structure of many schools has changed as, for example, with the changeover to comprehensive education and the abolition of the eleven-plus and the old binary system of secondary education. But these changes have in themselves, at the higher institutional level within the system, sped downwards into the normative and value system at their base, due to the continuous assessment of the effectiveness of experimental changes in terms of goal attainment.

Where new methods and institutional restructuring have failed to give satisfactory results this has inevitably led to the questioning and modification of values. Thus there is a continuous upward and downward effect of feedback within the system that has had the effect of stimulating the whole change process. But in a situation where the whole system is changing so rapidly that experimental models are set up one after the other with no time for proper assessment, evaluation and modification before the onslaught of the next wave of experimentation, the changes within the system are too great and too rapid to be absorbed. The result is a growing sense of a lack of clear goal definition amongst all the actors in the institution and a growing sense of dissatisfaction both amongst those in positions of responsibility for organization and administration, and for teachers and pupils. All alike feel equally caught up within the system and powerless to effect any influence upon the chain of events, whilst at the same time gaining less and less satisfaction from the institution and growing increasingly aware that their real interests are not being served.

Education, however, is not only subject to the forces of

change from within its own institutional boundaries. Interaction with other institutions within the total system also
plays its part in stoking up the change process and heighten-
ing the effect and the speed of the winds of change. Education
is subject to political decisions. These in turn are subject to
a change of direction when there is a change of government
– as, for example, when the Conservative Party took over
from Labour in 1979 and began to reverse the process of
changeover to comprehensive education and to reprieve the
grammar schools that were about to disappear. Education
has also been subject to interaction with the economy. The
economic recession of the late 1970s, coupled with the rising
level of unemployment, resulted in severe cutbacks in
the education budget, both nationally and through local
authorities. This brought about a shortage in the resources
available for education both in terms of materials, building
programmes and teaching staff. Political decisions were taken
to close some colleges of education, and further to reduce
the number of teachers available, thus creating anxiety and
frustration within the teaching profession – anxiety for job
security and frustration at the inadequacy of educational
facilities, resources and opportunities.

Changes in the family also affect education. Many schools
now have fifty per cent or more of their pupils coming from
one-parent families. Children from broken homes often do
not have the same educational opportunities as do children
from a conventional family home life. The co-operation of
the parent with the teachers, the parent's interest in the child,
and help given to the child's learning through the home life
is usually missing where the child lacks a stable family background. The family's attitudes towards educational achievement and to discipline and social order all affect the child's
performance at school. The radical changes that have, during
the past decade or so, taken place within the family in terms
of attitudes towards society, educational achievement and

social order have inevitably had their effect upon children and upon classroom standards of behaviour, and thereby upon the effectiveness of the whole educational process.

The changes in religion in Britain over the past twenty-five years have also had their effect upon education. The 1944 Act, which laid down that every child should receive religious education and participate in corporate worship, is now being widely observed in the breach. With fewer and fewer teachers having any strong Christian beliefs, a scripturally based act of worship or teaching programme is not possible in many schools. The influx into inner-city schools, as a result of migration from the New Commonwealth, of tens of thousands of children of other religious backgrounds has added to education the further complication of religious pluralism. Many schools are struggling to find a pluralistic, multi-faith style of corporate worship. Teaching programmes for R.E. have had to be drastically revised to take the form of either comparative religion or ethical studies. Tens of thousands of children now have no basic Christian teaching at all in British schools, and the day may not be too far away when a political decision will be taken to abolish the 1944 Act's provision for religious education for all children. Thus basic changes in religion have had their effect upon education.

It may be seen that the interaction between major institutions, as part of the total interaction process within the social system, has a considerable effect upon a major institution such as education. These interactions, coupled with the continuous process of change within education itself, leading upwards from the underlying values of education and downwards from the organizational structural level of education, are all producing changes that lead upwards and downwards and across the institutional boundaries. These changes stimulate other changes, and they work on the change processes that operate through the interaction between open systems, and across boundaries, in a vast chain reaction generating changes in response to the changes that are responses to the changes that result from the changes within institutional boundaries. In other words, what is being produced is a highly volatile situation!

Every change produces a multitude of change factors, each of which has spin-off effects that move in a variety of directions and each produces its own chain reaction of changes. It is like watching a firework display where the night sky is gradually filled with a multifarious pattern of ever changing shapes and colours, and where multi-stage rockets push out numerous balls of light, each of which explodes into a hundred smaller balls of light, each of which explodes again and so on, with the whole process being stoked up by the injection of further rockets so that the scene is continually changing and never allowed to settle in a regular pattern.

Shaking Social Foundations

The real danger facing us in Britain today is that the changes taking pace in the social structure are so radical and far reaching that they are fundamentally affecting the normative structure. They feed down into the value system upon which it rests and reciprocally back up again into the social structure at every point within the total social system. This is having the effect of generating an ever increasing rate of change in all parts of the total system, and through interaction within the system itself and across boundaries from one major social institution to another, so that the total social system is being affected more radically and fundamentally than at any other period in history.

This is a situation the outcome of which no social scientist can predict with any degree of accuracy, since it is a totally new phenomenon. It is, however, arguable that there is a level of change beyond which a society cannot go without running the risk of the total disintegration of its entire social system. Let us think of the social system in the form of a tower block that is undergoing enormous vibrations. The whole building is being shaken by an ever increasing velocity and intensity, as when an earthquake occurs, with vibrations being transmitted up from the foundations through to the very top of the building and bouncing back down through the structure of the building to hit oncoming waves of vibrations still being transmitted upwards from the foundations. This causes the building to shake even more violently, until the point is reached where the walls begin to crack and the whole structure disintegrates.

That is a reasonable picture of what is happening to our society. The vibrations from the changes in the value system are being reflected up through the substructure to the superstructure and bouncing down again to hit the shock waves of change that are still on their way up from the foundations. The substructure begins to shake ever more violently. There are increasing signs of cracks in the superstructure and evidence that the whole system is under increasing tension and strain and stress. The day of the collapse of the system cannot be too far delayed, so long as the inevitable process of change and effect, change and effect, change and yet more change continues unabated.

Perhaps the greatest source of danger is that while a great many people in Britain today recognize that there is something wrong with society, they are not at all sure just what is really happening. They see changes taking place around them but are unable to recognize or identify the processes of social change. They are therefore not in a position to be able to identify the real sources of danger of which they are only vaguely aware. On the other hand there are many sociologists who are perfectly well aware of the gathering momentum of the processes of social change that are shaking the foundations of society and chipping away at the stability of the total system, but they are unwilling to speak out about these dangers to the national life because of their own commitment to a philosophy of political revolution. Their political aspirations and objectives can be aided immensely by the kind of social disintegration towards which Britain is heading. They therefore have a vested interest in maintaining silence.

Despite the fact that what we are seeing in Britain is an entirely new set of social phenomena for a highly complex urban industrial society, on the basis of all that we know concerning the processes of social change and their effects upon social systems, it is possible to predict with a reasonable degree of accuracy the likely outcome if the present trends continue unabated. There can in fact only be one outcome and that is the disintegration of the entire social system. It will probably begin first with the normative structure and the breakdown of norms regulating social behaviour, with particular stress in the sphere of public law and order. The cracks in these boundaries will fairly rapidly spill over to all other social institutions, working upwards to bring down the entire superstructure of social organization. The disintegration of organized social life or civilization as we have known it in Britain for the past hundred years or so cannot long be delayed.

The danger of this occurring is intensified by the fact that most people, although having a vague sense of unease that all is not well with the national life, have no idea of the magnitude of the danger facing us today. We are like the citizens of Pompeii going about their ordinary domestic and social affairs entirely oblivious of the catastrophe about to erupt over their city. A mountain of molten lava descended upon them so quickly, and with such a mighty avalanche, that it engulfed all the inhabitants of that great city as they went about the ordinary business of their daily life. The entire city was caught unawares and was destroyed in the twinkling of an eye. What is happening in Britain is like the relentless tide hammering away at the base of the cliff, gradually eroding the foundations of the rock upon which the land mass above is supported. All looks well above ground, apart from the occasional crack. Then one wild and stormy night, with the wind at gale force, driving rain and mountainous seas, there is a mighty crash and the entire cliff – rocks, subsoil and soil – slides down into the engulfing waters below.

This will be the fate of Britain unless . . .

Creative Social Change

If we are right in looking to the value system as the fundamental source of all social change, then we have a key of immense significance for understanding what is happening in Britain today and for the formulation of creative policies of social change that may save our nation from the inevitability of destruction if the present forces are allowed to continue unabated.

Parsons states that the values of a society normally change only very slowly, but what we have seen in Britain is a comparatively rapid period of change. These changes have occurred very largely because of basic changes in the traditional religious belief system in Britain since the beginning of this century. This has been due both to the rapid advances of Biblical liberalism during this period and to similar advances in the process of secularization. Liberalism has undermined the faith of Biblical scholars and preachers, while secularization has aided the onslaught of secularism that has led to the undermining of the faith of ordinary lay Christians. The Church has gone out into the world, as bidden in scripture, to engage in every aspect of life in order to sanctify (or make holy) the whole of life, but in so doing it has left the doors open so wide that the world has slipped into the

Church. The result has been the secularization of religion rather than the sanctification of the secular.

As the twentieth century has progressed so an increasing number of theological colleges have turned out into the ministry men with no Biblical certainty as the basis of their faith. If preachers don't believe the scriptures they preach – and this is true of a large number of clergy and ministers, including those in positions of high responsibility in all the major denominations – then how can their preaching have any sincerity and conviction? 'If the bugle gives an indistinct sound, who will get ready for battle?' asks Paul (1 Corinthians 14:8). It is small wonder that the faith of the faithful concentrates on the few things about which they are certain – the norms of Christian behaviour, such as doing good to our neighbours, showing concern for the Third World and for the underprivileged, raising money for Christian Aid, fighting for racial justice and a host of other good causes that are a valid part of the concerns of a Christian society *but are not the basis of its faith.* Much of what comes from Christian pulpits today has nothing whatever to do with the Gospel! It is at best Christian ethics. It is at worst a kind of vague humanism.

The Gospel in essence is incredibly simple. It simply states that man is a sinner who because of his sins is separated from God both in this life and in the next, but that God has broken down the barriers of separation through the life, the death and the resurrection of Jesus Christ. Man has only to accept Jesus as Lord to enter into a new relationship with God and to participate in a new realm of spiritual living that changes the whole basis of life.

As the twentieth century has progressed, this simple basis of faith has gradually disappeared as the main thrust of Christian proclamation and the major *raison d'être* of the Church. Hence with the onslaught of secularism in the advance of a technological society, and with the increasing urbanization of society and thus the movement away from the land and from the world of nature and natural resources, the values of society have undergone radical change.

These values have been changing rapidly at the very point in time at which the greatest advances in technology in the whole history of mankind have been achieved. These technological advances have inevitably necessitated changes in the whole social organization of life.

If ever there was a time when we needed the stability of constant, unchanging values at the foundations of our society it is during this period of massive and radical change! It is as though there were a gigantic cosmic plot undertaken by the forces of darkness, forces that Paul speaks of as the 'principalities and powers', the cosmic forces of evil. At a critical point in history they have moved in on our society with a devastating consequence. They have, from the realm of ultimate reality, been feeding into the value system that undergirds the total social system, forces designed to change the values of society. They have done it in such a way and at such a time that there are no certainties, no yardsticks, no basic principles to provide a compass point of reference by which the changes occurring in society could be evaluated and on the basis of which they could either be rejected, modified or accepted. Without such a yardstick all is uncertainty and the result is chaos. This is exactly the nature of the chaos we have been experiencing, with mounting gravity, throughout the past twenty-five years.

With no certain basis to the values of society and an ever increasing rate of change in the normative structure and in social organization, chaos is inevitable and the end result in terms of mounting chaos, normative anarchy, the breakdown of social organization and the final disintegration of the entire system is equally inevitable.

Christian Responsibility

If we are right in our analysis of the primary sources of social change being rooted in the value system, then Christians above all others have an enormous weight of responsibility upon them. Again, if Christians are right in believing that they have in Jesus Christ God's ultimate revelation of himself to mankind, then there is laid upon them with the utmost urgency the necessity of proclaiming this revelation of God's truth to a generation that is heading for a Sodom and Gomorrah type of destruction of our civilization. Christians have the responsibility for feeding into the system the fundamental sources of creative change that God has put into their hands. The Christian understanding of the Logos as God's creative power, through which the world and all its inhabitants were formed and through whom God also carried out his purpose of releasing man from the grip of the forces that were threatening to destroy mankind and of bringing him into new life, this understanding is the one hope of saving our civilization today. If our sociological analysis is correct then our entire national way of life is threatened with disintegration. *There is only one power that can save it, only one power that is able to intervene at the real source of creative social change, and that is the power of God the Creator – the spiritual power that he has made available to us that can redirect the course of history and save Britain from destruction.* The problems we see in society are the mere phenomenology of what is fundamentally a spiritual problem – a sickness in the value system at the foundations of society. It is primarily a spiritual problem rather than a social problem, in the sense that it can only be dealt with by spiritual means and not by social organization or by manipulative adjustments of the social order.

The task lying ahead is one of enormous responsibility for

Christians. If we do not seize this opportunity there may never be another.

Christians have the opportunity of bringing new life to a dying nation. But the task is urgent – very urgent indeed. We are probably nearer to the point of no return, the point at which the whole system goes spinning out of control, or, to revert to our earlier metaphor of the building during an earthquake, the point at which the building starts to shake so violently that the main structural walls begin to crumble – we are probably nearer to that point than the most expert social analysts would care to admit.

Can we put a date on it? No, there are too many variables and uncertainties. But it is coming soon. It will not be long delayed.

POLITICAL AND ECONOMIC FACTORS

A nation without God's guidance is a nation
without order.

> Proverbs 29:18
> (Good News Bible)

CHAPTER FOUR

POLITICAL AND ECONOMIC FACTORS

British people have never taken easily to change. There is something essentially conservative about the British character – we admire stability, we despise instability. For generations a major value in our national life has been the preservation of the *status quo*. Hence the ethos of one of our major political parties has always been to resist change and to preserve what is traditional in our national heritage.

One of the most fascinating facets of the British character is that while social class dominates our national life, attitudes towards change are not determined by it. This is one of the factors about the British character that foreigners find impossible to understand. Ordinary working people with little or no stake in the national wealth or the means of production are essentially just as conservative in their attitudes towards change as are the traditional aristocracy. The most violent form of change is political revolution. It is, of course, a well known sociological fact that revolutions rarely stem from the working classes. They arise from the lower middle classes, or petty bourgeoisie, whose social aspirations are blocked due to a variety of impedimenta in the social structure. The essential conservatism of the British working classes, plus the relatively small size of the petty bourgeoisie, have accounted for the fact that since becoming an industrial society Britain has not so far experienced a revolution.

Social class is a product of industrialization, and as a concept is predictable only of an industrial society. Hence in a pre-industrial society we may speak of 'social ranks' but not of social classes. In the early days of the industrial revolution in Britain, when the embryonic forms of the middle classes were just beginning to emerge, class differences in terms of attitudes towards social change were already discernible. It was the rising artisan classes who were in the vanguard of change. It was their spirit of adventure, their quest for knowledge and their inventive genius that produced the new technology, which in turn made it possible to revolutionize the means of production. It was not the aristocracy, or the landed gentry, the traditional elites of society, who were in the advance guard of the changes, changes that were to bring new wealth to the nation, new productivity and a new way of life that would eventually sweep away all the traditions of hundreds of years of feudalism.

Equally it was not the peasant workers who were leading the changes or were heralding their advent with joy. They were, in fact, as conservative as their traditional masters. Each new advance in technology that changed the mode of production was regarded as an omen of death rather than as the sign of new life in the economy of the nation.

Gradually the changes were introduced that moved Britain inexorably from a feudal agrarian economy to a labour-intensive industrial economy. Gradually the village crafts disappeared, superceded by the steam-powered machines of the factory. As the home-based hand loom became obsolete with the rise of the power looms in the mill factories, whole villages were faced with social disaster. People either starved or they made their way into the new townships that were arising around the factories and sold the only commodity they had to offer – the labour of their bodies. They found shelter in the houses provided by their new masters, who controlled the rents of their homes as well as the wages they were paid.

The owners of industry determined the hours they worked and the conditions of their servitude. Thus a new class of 'urban peasants' arose, the landless poor, who didn't even have a tiny plot on which to grow their own vegetables or to keep a goat or pig and who had no access to common grazing ground for a sheep or a cow. They were utterly dependent upon their new masters for their entire subsistence. They were the new urban slaves, essentially the product of industrialization. Yet it was their misery that brought gladness and prosperity to the rising new middle classes.

It was small wonder that the peasant workers loathed the changes of the new order with as much intensity as did their feudal overlords. The major difference in conservatism between that of the elites and that of the rural peasants was that the elites possessed the resources to withstand the onslaught upon their power, prestige and privilege for a prolonged period, whereas the poor did not. They faced immediate starvation as the means of their livelihood disappeared. For the rich it was a galling sight to witness the rise of the *nouveau riche*, as the national source of wealth moved inevitably away from the ownership of land to the ownership of the means of production. Those who were sufficiently far-sighted and who were prepared to accept the inevitability of the changes in the economy were able to invest in the new economic enterprises. Thus there arose a new class of entrepreneurs.

Those who were unprepared to accept the reality of the changes settled down in their country seats and prepared themselves for a long siege – to resist the changes for as long as possible. No such luxury was afforded to the poor. They had no hidden assets, no invested reserves. As the village crafts disappeared so did their ability to survive. It is small wonder that in their desperation many of them turned and attacked the new machines that symbolized the destruction of the old way of life and which had led to their present plight. 'The

Luddites', as they became known, arose around 1815. They were so named after one Ned Ludd who led a mob of peasants who smashed up machinery in the mills where the introduction of power looms was making hand loom weavers redundant. Similar outbreaks of violence occurred in many parts of the country around this period.

The rise of the Luddites brought about a change in the law that was very basic in terms of human freedom in Britain. Hurried through Parliament in order to deal effectively with the perpetrators of these disturbances that threatened the new material prosperity of the owners of industry, the new law made it a capital offence to damage or destroy machinery. The sentence could, at the discretion of the magistrates, be reduced to deportation. The effect of the new law was to put on to the statute book of Britain a regulation that made it explicit that *machinery was of more value than life*. Thus the spirit of the new age of materialism had dawned! It was the moment in which Britain changed her gods. Machines mattered more than men and prosperity was more important than life.

We are today entering a new phase in the transition of the economy – the technological revolution. The changes it will bring to the economy, to the means of production and to the character of social life in Britain and throughout the industrial world, will be just as revolutionary as was that of the original industrial revolution some two hundred years ago.

During the 1980s we may expect to see sweeping changes take place in almost every sphere of life, due to the advances in technology that are now being made. We have already entered the age of the computer, but it is the micro-computer and the development of micro-electronics that represent the real source of economic change. It is now possible to programme a computer to control all the machinery in a factory so that the whole production process can be automated, thus making the machine-minder of today as redundant as was the hand loom operator in the early nineteenth century. We are within sight of the end of the era of labour-intensive production. We thus stand poised on the edge of an era of enormous social change that will affect not only the basic means of production of consumer goods but the whole of our way of life. This change will affect us not simply in terms of our occupations or economic pursuits but also in every other aspect of our social being, from the mode of transportation to the choice of leisure pursuits and even to the basic structure of our family and community life.

The reason we may offer such a confident prediction of far reaching social changes during the closing decades of the twentieth century is based on all that we know of the theory of social change. As we saw in chapter 3, in any society there are five major social institutions, the Family, the Economy, Education, Law and Government, and Religion.

A radical change in any one of these five will result in changes in each of the others. Thus the new technology of the eighteenth century, which changed the basis of the economy from an agrarian to a labour-intensive production mechanism, also changed all the other major social institutions. The changes in the economy uprooted families and resettled them in an urban environment. This affected the basic structure of the family. From an economically inter-dependent unit with a common purse, sharing common values, beliefs and life style and carrying out the socialization of its own young, the family changed to an economically independent social group, with individual wages earned in different enterprises through which each individual was exposed to different social values, beliefs and life styles, and in which the formal socialization of the young was carried out in institutions separated from the family.

We noted this point in the previous chapter where we examined in some detail the effects of social change on different aspects of our social life. For the moment the relevance of noting the 'spin off' effects of changes in any one major social institution is that it underlines the contention that we are moving into an extremely turbulent period of social change, due to the radical nature of the changes now occurring in the economy. These changes will undoubtedly be strenuously resisted by many, and in particular by those workers whose labour will be made redundant. We have, in fact, already witnessed the opening salvoes of this struggle. This was one of the factors underlying the struggle between workers and management on *The Times*. It followed the installation of new machinery that would carry out automatically part of the type-setting process previously done by men in the printing trade. They saw their skills being made obsolete and their livelihoods threatened. The same thing is happening throughout industry, and with the introduction of new technology that renders labour-intensive methods of production obsolete, there have been attacks on machinery in precisely the same way as the Luddites reacted to the introduction of power-driven machinery in the early nineteenth century.

We may expect to see an increasing intensity of the struggle against the introduction of the new technology that threatens the livelihood of millions of workers. This struggle will affect every aspect of social life. Already there are demands for work-sharing schemes that would give each worker a three-day working week and that would allow two men to be employed instead of one. Such a practice, if widely introduced, would have a radical effect on family life It would elevate the importance of leisure-time pursuits and soon every aspect of social life would be affected, including our social values and religious beliefs and practices. The changes would be reflected in law and the political life of the nation, as well as in education, so that in time all our major social institutions would be affected.

But social change never does take place smoothly as an unbroken process of transition. The changes that we are likely to witness during the next twenty years may well be of such cataclysmic intensity that by comparison the changes introduced by the industrial revolution of the eighteenth and nineteenth centuries will pale into insignificance. Although there are certain similarities between the situation in the early nineteenth century and that of today, there are other vital and basic differences that make our present situation infinitely more dangerous to social stability. Today both management and labour are highly organized, and each side understands the other's objectives, strengths and limitations in a way totally unknown a hundred and fifty or two hundred years ago.

The leaders of labour know perfectly well that the entrepreneurs who control the means of production are in business to maximize profit and not to run charitable institutions. If that is overstating the case we may at least assert with some confidence that the principle underlying a capitalist system is to get the best return on an investment, and when this is applied to a production process it means that the cost of production must be kept to a minimum in order to produce the end product as cheaply as possible so that it may be sold on the market at a maximum profit. Thus if a computer-controlled production process can produce goods much more cheaply than a labour-intensive production process it will obviously be preferred by entrepreneurs in a capitalist system. The fact that it would render countless jobs obsolete would be irrelevant, unless the restricted purchasing power of the workers diminished the market for consumer goods to such an extent that the price dropped and profitability was affected. This, of course, would create slump conditions, which are feared equally by the entrepreneur and by the worker.

No doubt in an enlightened society, where individual greed

and avarice were controlled by an overriding concern for the welfare of the whole society and where each individual's place within that society was equally valued, this basic economic problem could be solved. In a society in which there was a real desire to share the national wealth, while at the same time harnessing advances in technology to increase gross productivity, economic problems would fall into place once the basic social ethos of a caring, sharing society was established. Men and women could be liberated from the economic enslavement of routine production processes in a labour-intensive system. They could in time be retrained for filling different roles in society which would be more fulfilling and satisfying than machine-minding in a factory. One example is that there could be a massive expansion of the creative arts, leisure-time pursuits, educational and service industries. This would allow for a shorter working week with an increase in, rather than a loss of, income, through a sharing of the increased wealth derived from the increased gross national profit resulting from the application of advanced technology to the production processes.

All this is but a vain utopian dream unless the ideology of a caring, sharing society is established as one of the foundation values of the nation. To establish such a value in the life of the nation requires a basic change in the very nature of man which can only be effected spiritually, i.e. by a radical change in the spiritual nature of man that changes his attitude towards his fellows and thereby his social and economic values. But such a basic spiritual change cannot be engendered in mankind *en masse*. It can only be transmitted to each man individually, and this change is the work of the Holy Spirit in each individual. It is not something that man can achieve for himself, it is something only God can do, because he is the creator of our spiritual being and only he can engender a radical change within it. Such a transformation is what the Christian theologians call 'an act of grace' and not of merit. It is something only God can do for us. We cannot do it for ourselves.

God's pre-condition for changing man's spiritual nature is man's repentance. This in itself presupposes man's recognition of his need, and his turning to God for help in penitence and humility. There is no alternative open to man. God has left him no other choice. Man either chooses to ask for God to renew his spiritual nature, and thereby to give him new life through Christ, or he is inexorably driven by the forces that are at work in our society. Those forces are driving us towards a period of revolutionary change in our social and economic life that will unleash unprecedented forces of violence and destruction within the life of our nation. We are thus quite literally faced with the choice of life or death. We either choose new life in Christ or we are driven by the forces of death and destruction.

The Christian prophet today – like the great eighth-century BC prophets who foretold impending destruction due to the social and economic corruption in the life of the nation – has to declare a similar message to the people of Britain. There is an inevitability in the destruction that lies ahead of us. Yet at the same time, like the prophets of old who proclaimed the word of the Lord to the people, we also offer a message of hope and new life in the name of the Lord, if men will but hear it and turn from their evil ways. If they refuse to hear, and continue on their present course, then both management and labour will be swept away in the resulting turmoil. The economic analysis of Marx and Engels should be studied as carefully by the entrepreneurs and the middle management of a capitalist system as it is by the devotees of the 'new Left'.

Marx declares with penetrating perception that capitalism is a necessary phase in the development of an egalitarian society. Capitalism was needed to break the power of a feudal society that had reigned supreme and unchallengeable for hundreds of years. Capitalism, having destroyed the feudal structure of society, then set about instituting an alternative social structure that contained within itself the seeds of its own destruction. It institutionalized the class war: 'a struggle between the proletariat and the bourgeoisie', between the wage labourers and the owners of the means of production in industry.

Instead of sharing out the rich profits of the new processes of mass production, the owners of industry took most for themselves and paid their helpless workers slave wages. The grinding poverty of the poor thus established the aggressive nature of the relationship between capital and labour. In so doing the capitalists, according to Marx, sowed the seeds of their own destruction by making it necessary for wage labourers to organize their own associations for their defence and for the promotion of their own interests. Marx believed that the organization of labour would result in a gradual increase in its power until the point was reached where they would be able to carry out a successful revolution and wrest political as well as economic power away from the ruling classes. He writes, 'the essential condition for the existence and for the sway of the bourgeois class, is the formation and the augmentation of capital; the condition for capital is wage labour. Wage labour rests exclusively on competition between the labourers. The advance of industry, whose involuntary promoter is the bourgeoisie, replaces the isolation of the labourers, due to competition, by their revolutionary combination, due to association. The development of modern industry, therefore, cuts from under its feet the very foundation on which the bourgeoisie produces and appropriates products. What the bourgeoisie therefore produces, above all, are its own gravediggers. Its fall and the victory of the proletariat are equally inevitable.'[20]

Marx is perfectly right in forecasting a change in the role

of organized labour. This can clearly be discerned in the changes that have taken place in the Trades Union movement over the past hundred and fifty years. In the early days of Friendly Societies they were associations of craftsmen or of artisans plying similar trades. The purpose underlying each association was the legitimate advancement of that craft or trade. Gradually the associations took upon themselves the role of economic negotiation or bargaining with management. This was, for a period, strenuously resisted by many owners, who refused to negotiate with representatives, preferring to agree a wage with each individual worker separately thus maintaining their own control of wages and working conditions. This struggle has not entirely disappeared from the British industrial scene, as the prolonged Grunwick dispute in 1978 amply demonstrated. Gradually over the past hundred years organized labour through the Trades Union movement has increasingly entered the political realm. At first this was through the support of Labour Party candidates at Parliamentary elections, although when first introduced this was strenuously resisted by many leaders within the Trades Union movement. It was only at the third attempt that a majority vote for such a policy was secured at the Trades Union Congress in 1899.

Today the political activities of trades unions are not confined to the support of Parliamentary candidates, neither are their political aspirations confined to the institution of Parliamentary democracy. As Marx rightly forecast, they have today entered a new phase of political activity in pursuance of the struggle between the proletariat and the bourgeoisie, or organized labour and the ruling classes. This is seen in the political activities of the rank and file trade unionists who, often in defiance of their own union leaders, enter into dispute with management in industry. This is part of a long term strategy of industrial warfare now being waged by the militant new Left, with the ultimate objective of wresting political power to themselves.

The new Left consist of a consortium of Marxists, Leninists, Maoists, Trotskyites and various kinds of revolutionaries who go under a variety of banners such as 'The International Socialists', 'The Socialist Workers' Party', 'The Workers' Revolutionary Party' and others representing smaller groups. The I.S., the S.W.P., the W.R.P. and fellow travellers are all basically Marxist in philosophy and unite under a single political objective: that of breaking the power of organized capital and placing it in the hands of the workers. Together they represent the new Left.

The strategy at present being pursued by the new Left is the infiltration of rank and file membership of trades unions in every section of industry, with the objective of dictating policy in labour/management relationships. That policy is to create as much disruption as possible to the production process. The objective of the disruption of industry is to promote the eventual economic collapse of the country, so that normal political processes of government become impossible. This will then give the new Left the opportunity to strike a political blow that will place the power of government firmly in the hands of the workers.

By using the economy as the primary agent to pave the way for a political revolution, that will in turn achieve a basic change in the social structure of Britain, the new Left are doing two things.

1. In the first place they are using the tools most readily at hand. As workers engaged in industry the only major commodity they have to offer is their labour. In a labour-intensive production system the weapon that on its own can hurt capital the most is the withdrawal of labour, resulting in the seizing up of production. By inciting the workers to withdraw their labour on the slightest pretext, the new Left are both undermining the economic stability of industry and

also causing maximum dislocation of the whole organization of capital.

2. In the second place the new Left are following out basic Marxist doctrine, which believes that the economy is the fundamental source of social creativity. The basis of Marxist doctrines is that the type of economy determines the type of society, i.e. that the social structure is determined by the nature of the economy of each society. The only way to change the social structure is to change the type of economy – hence the belief that the only way to achieve an egalitarian society is through changing from a capitalist economy to a communist economy.

This simplistic belief, which ignores some fundamental theoretical concepts of sociology (Marx was not a sociologist and hated sociologists as agents of bourgeois imperialism), overlooks the role and function of values in the structure of society. It ignores the fundamentally creative role of religious and moral beliefs and values as agents in social change as, for example, during the period of the Reformation.

The new Left, however, have a simplistic approach to the problem of social change. They are not concerned with the complexities of value orientation, neither do they reflect upon the sobering thought that an economic revolution leaves the nature of man untouched. Unchanged men, whether they be drawn from the proletariat or the bourgeoisie, are essentially greedy, self-centred and potentially violent and cruel when they find themselves in positions of power in society. The tragedy of the Russian Revolution, which produced from the proletariat a man such as Stalin, who must rank high amongst the world's cruellest dictators, is still doggedly ignored amongst Marxist doctrinaires. To the Christian it seems a simple enough dogma that unchanged men cannot create changed societies, but the new Left are not prepared to consider such fundamental truths.

Recent strikes in a number of industries underline the

clear political intention of the new Left. Whereas at one time the strike weapon was the final resort in the armoury of negotiators attempting to get better pay and conditions for their members, today many strikes have nothing whatsoever to do with such fundamental issues. They are motivated not by economic necessity, but by the desire for political advantage. They believe quite simply that by disrupting industry they will shake the economy, that when the economy is sufficiently weakened the political system will crumble, and that out of the mêlée the new Left will emerge triumphant.

The situation is, however, not quite so simple as this since the new Left are only one of the new political stars in the sky. We have also to reckon with the rise of the new Right, and what we are today witnessing is the polarization of political extremes of a nature hitherto unknown in Britain. Despite being polar-opposites in terms of representing opposing wings of the political chicken, there are some striking similarities between the new Right and the new Left, both in terms of objectives and of methodology.

The new Right are a consortium of right-wing extremists bringing together under a common umbrella such disparate groups as the Mosleyites and the anti-immigration organizations.

The Mosleyites are the remnants of the 1930s black-shirt followers of Sir Oswald Mosley, one-time admirer of the Italian dictator Mussolini, hence their derisory denigration as 'fascists' by their opponents on the extreme Left. Anti-immigration groups such as the 'Keep Britain White Campaign', together with 'The League of Empire Loyalists', the Mosleyites and similar groups, have today joined forces under the political umbrella organization of the 'National Front'. The N.F., like the new Left, thrive in areas of social deprivation. It is in such areas that black immigrants from the New Commonwealth have largely settled. It was here that they were able to find the two things they sought in Britain,

unskilled or semi-skilled employment, and housing accommodation within their limited means. Both these commodities
are in short supply in many inner-city areas, where social
deprivation is most intense, and it is in such areas that the
National Front capitalize upon the competition for scarce
resources to propagate their doctrines of racial hatred and
to fan into flames the fear of foreigners latent in every
Britisher. In all such areas N.F. wall slogans abound. Their
racist literature is freely distributed, their public meetings
are held in schools and town halls and their demonstrations
go through the streets.

The deliberate policy of the N.F. in recent years has been
to link immigration with unemployment – the two most
explosive issues in modern British politics. This was amply
demonstrated in June 1976 in Newham, in the East End of
London, where unemployment was rising steadily and at a
time of year when large numbers of school leavers were
swelling the ranks of the jobless. The I.S. decided to hold
a march through the streets of Newham, to demonstrate
against government policy that was giving rise to increasing
numbers of unemployed, and to show their concern at the
unacceptable level of unemployment. The march was to
begin in West Ham, go through East Ham, and end in a
park in the north-east of the borough. As soon as plans for
the march were made public the N.F. decided to hold a
counter-demonstration – along the same route, at the same
time, on the same Saturday afternoon, starting at the same
point and finishing at the same point as the I.S. march. The
objective of the N.F. march was to demonstrate against
government policy on immigration, and to express concern
against what they considered to be the unacceptably high
numbers of immigrants in Britain. The march was clearly
highly provocative and was a direct challenge to the new
Left. The N.F. were making a deliberate attempt to link
unemployment with immigration.

The police had no hesitation in telling the N.F. that they could not follow the same route, but they would not, however, ban the march. They allowed it to start at the same time from a point not too far distant from the anti-unemployment march, but taking a different route and moving towards a different spot. In the event a squad of youths from the N.F. march left their own demonstration and made their way to the park where the left-wing demonstration was due to rally. They were met by police with riot shields and helmets, who stood between the two groups of demonstrators. There was some rock-throwing, followed by street scuffles extending over several hours, and at the end of this day an eighteen-year-old white boy lay dying on the pavement from a stab wound. Which side he was on, or whether he had even been a participant in either of the demonstrations, was never made clear but his death symbolized in a tragic way the plight of the poor and the powerless in our decaying inner-city areas. It is they who are suffering from all the disadvantages of social deprivation, poor education, low standards of housing, lack of social amenities, a drab decaying environment, high unemployment, no career prospects, plus the high prices for consumer goods constantly flaunted before them by an advertising-dominated, materialistic, affluent society.

These are the classic conditions for creating high levels of relative deprivation. Deprivation is not an *absolute*, it is always *relative*. There is no absolute standard of subsistence below which a man cannot survive, for what would sustain life in one society or climate would be impossible in another. Deprivation is based upon how we see ourselves *in relation to others*. The 'others' with whom we compare ourselves (in theoretical terms, our 'comparative reference group') are our peer group within our own society. Young people growing up in inner-city areas and possessing low standards of education, with no qualifications to enable them to obtain employment, and who see other young people receiving high wages and enjoying all the benefits of a consumer society, feel deeply resentful that they themselves are denied access to the kind of things in life that are available to others in their peer group.

It is small wonder that they feel bewildered and frustrated. They are taught to want things and to expect certain things in life, by the mindless advertising slogans of a television-crazy generation, and yet the very same society which teaches them to want these materialistic social values also denies them access to them. Is it any wonder that the young inner-city, unemployed, socially deprived youths grow up with anti-social attitudes and engage in anti-social behaviour? These same youths, are, moreover, an easy prey for the purveyors of political extremism. Right and Left, each are equally anxious to enlist their support. Both the new Left and the new Right are minority movements and anti-Establishment, with a consequent easy appeal to youth and especially to those experiencing social rejection. To belong to a party that hates the established form of government and opposes the oppressors offers a welcome opportunity to hit back at those who are responsible for the society that has rejected you.

Both political extremes are also prepared to use violent means in order to achieve their ends. Such a philosophy makes a ready appeal to deprived youths brought up in an inner-city environment in which violence is commonplace. To be offered the opportunity of using their violent urges in a noble cause is like a gift from the gods. To march through the streets in a large company, and to shout slogans with the possibility of a legitimate punch-up against 'hate figures' is an exciting prospect for an inner-city youth. It breaks the drab monotony of inner-city life more effectively than does the prospect of a punch-up with the supporters of the opposing football team on the terraces of Upton Park, or the Den or the Cop, or the Stretford end of Old Trafford. An additional thrill is when police intervention gives the opportunity for rock-throwing, or for an actual hand-to-hand punch-up against the traditional hated enemy of the working classes: the forces of law and order – the men in blue!

For many inner-city youths the choice of which side they support, N.F. or I.S., is a matter of who gets to them first. This is undoubtedly one of the reasons why the N.F. have been strenuously pushing their literature in schools in many inner-city areas in recent years. To many white inner-city youths they offer the additio. l bonus of being anti-black. This provides a scapegoat for the youth labouring under a sense of personal failure. It also gives him a target for his hatred. It is difficult to hate society at large when you are labouring under a sense of rejection and deprivation. It is much easier if you can identify the target. You then know who to blame and who to hate. The N.F. provide just this: 'There are too many blacks in Britain. Send them back!' Their racist lies find ready ears amongst the deprived in the back streets of our inner cities, which fester and ferment with all the social ills generated by a decaying civilization. 'Don't blame the blacks, blame the bosses,' counter the Marxists. The new Left try vainly to unite workers of all races against the real enemy – the ruling classes, the unseen, faceless capitalists who control their lives by the ownership of industry. 'Join us and fight the *real* enemy – the ruling classes.' Such is the urgent appeal of the new Left to inner-city youth. For those who do join them there is always the happy prospect of a practice punch-up with the N.F. while they are awaiting the day when they take on the real enemy, the ruling classes.

The N.F. are seen as the fascist pawns in the hands of the ruling classes, the petty tyrants who if they gained power would show an even more unacceptable face of capitalism than that of the present rulers. The 'fascist jack-boots' have to be stopped, as they threaten the freedom of the workers. The capitalist rulers of Europe did nothing in the '30s to stop the rise of Hitler and Mussolini, and they eventually paid the price of their own indolence. The workers of Britain must see to it that it does not happen again. They must crush the fascists with force. They must act now before the Nazis become too strong and pose a real threat to the plans of the proletariat.

It is heady stuff! It appeals strongly to those suffering from high levels of relative deprivation.

There are many forms of social deprivation – economic deprivation, status deprivation, ethnic deprivation, to name but three. The inner-city youth in today's Britain is suffering from all of them. This makes him utterly vulnerable to this kind of revolutionary propaganda, with the additional attractive prospects of a position of some social significance in the 'new order' that will follow the successful revolution. When the workers are in control he will no longer be a nobody. He will be a somebody. Those who at present despise and reject him as having no social significance will have to take notice of him. He will have power! The new Left appeal strongly to the youth suffering from social deprivation – just as strongly as do the new Right. The factors that determine which side any particular youth will join are probably insignificant, factors such as the strength of racist attitudes he has internalized from home or school or neighbourhood peer group, or simply which side has got to him first. Both sides offer him similar activities, excitement and the prospects of power in the new order.

A significant development in the polarization of political extremes that has been taking place in recent years is the growth of organization and the growing strength of determination in the pursuance of their policies. The Newham confrontation of 1976 paled almost into insignificance the following year, with the massive disturbance in Lewisham, euphemistically termed 'The Battle of Lewisham High Street' by the press. My wife was at that time employing a team of youths under a Job Creation Scheme, rebuilding a semi-derelict church and transforming it into a Christian com-

munity centre. One of these lads lost an eye in the battle
of Lewisham. We never did find out which side he was
fighting on at the time, although we suspected he was with
the National Front since he had earlier been involved in rock-
throwing incidents at passing Pakistanis around the site of
the old church. He may have simply gone for the prospect
of a punch-up with the police. Probably it didn't matter
anyway which side he was on, since neither side could really
claim a victory and the only losers were the police and the
cause of law and order. His loss of an eye gained him considerable status in the local neighbourhood gang-land, where
battle scars are honourable indications of manly virility.

Lewisham in its turn was small-scale in terms of organization (although not in terms of violence) in comparison with
subsequent demonstrations such as that of Manchester 1978.
The really significant factor about these demonstrations is
the opportunity they give for the expression of anti-social
attitudes and behaviour. The real threat to social stability
comes not, however, from the new Right but from the new
Left. The Right simply represent the repressed rage and
frustration of an age that has lost world social significance.
Those who feel most keenly the loss of empire are those who
themselves suffer from a high level of personal status deprivation. They transpose their own failure to achieve in society
on to the rulers of the nation who have given away the
colonies – symbol of the pride of our race, source of our wealth
and birthright of every true-born Britisher. They pose as the
defenders of tradition, of all that is 'British' in our national
way of life, of law and order, of social values and morality.
As such they make their appeal to those for whom life in
modern Britain holds little prospect.

The polarization of political extremes is a phenomenon
linked with social deprivation, and occurs in areas of intense
social stress. For instance, in Newham two fairly middle of
the road traditional Labour Members of Parliament have

been fighting opposite battles. In the North East constituency of the borough Reg Prentice throughout the '70s fought a losing battle against the onslaught of the new Left, who eventually forced his resignation from the party and then ensured that his safe Labour seat went to a supporter of the new Left. At the opposite end of the borough Nigel Spearing was fighting for his seat against the new Right. Each time he defended the seat he faced the largest vote for a National Front candidate in Britain, a vote that forced the Conservatives into third place. The growing power and influence of the N.F. in a traditional dockland Labour strong-hold is one of the most puzzling political phenomena of our modern age, and is understandable only in terms of its relationship to social deprivation in the area.

The real danger from the N.F. lies not so much in their ability to win seats at the polls or in their potential revolutionary threat to the social order. It lies in the opposition they engender not simply from the new Left but from a wide range of other groups and individuals who abhor racism. In the closing years of the 1970s the rise of the 'Anti-Nazi League' is one of the outstanding political and social events of the decade. And it may well prove to be the most significant development of the 1970s in terms of the spark that has been lit. The A.N.L. has brought together under a single umbrella a hotchpotch of idealists, together with doctrinaire Marxists and the riff-raff of inner-city lads of violence. The idealists include intellectuals of many different political persuasions who hate racism, and Christians from different traditions and denominational backgrounds who wish to oppose racism and who bear witness to their belief in the name of Christ who died for all men, a gospel of universal love. They believe in one Father of the whole family of mankind, who breaks down all racial distinctions, and one Saviour in whom 'There is neither Jew nor Greek, there is neither slave nor free, there is neither male nor female' (Galatians 3:28).

The idealists also include anarchists and Quakers, liberals and conservatives, immigrant leaders from every segment of the community, lecturers and church-men, rich and poor, all who wish to be good neighbours with their new neighbours and who want to demonstrate their abhorrence of racial hatred. The new Left have eagerly seized this great new opportunity to marshal these unexpected allies under the banner of the defence of freedom, against the 'jack-boots of the Nazis'. The Marxists are thus able to pose as the upholders of democracy and the defenders of the sacred right of every individual, regardless of race or colour, to the privileges of citizenship in a democratic way of life. At the same time they are able to use the lads of violence for frontal attacks upon N.F. supporters. Consequent disturbances help to disrupt normal social life, to undermine the morale of the police, to pose further threats to the maintenance of law and order, and to give valuable experience in the use of communal violence against the day when the real revolution takes place.

There is great danger in this consortium of idealists who go under the banner of the Anti-Nazi League in their association with the Marxists. Many of the idealists are probably quite unaware of the extent to which they are being used by the forces of the new Left, by whom they are seen as welcome allies in the struggle against imperialism and capitalism. The dangers of Christians joining in Anti-Nazi League demonstrations were clearly expressed by a Christian who attended one such demonstration. In an unpublished report entitled 'Should Christians Support the Anti-Nazi League?' he wrote:

On Sunday 24 September 1978 between 60,000 and 100,000 people joined the second Anti-Nazi League Carnival in London. The huge crowd marched from Hyde Park to Brixton where they were entertained by rock music and side shows in Brockwell Park. The large numbers involved indicate that the Anti-Nazi League (A.N.L.) is a significant mass movement, a political force which has succeeded in capturing the imagination and allegiance of large numbers of people. As the *Morning Star* said in its editorial the following day: 'The Anti-Nazi League, with the spreading range of movements under its general umbrella, is now a major force to be reckoned with. It is the duty of all in the Labour movement, in the religious organizations and churches, in the broad popular movements, in work places, and in every town and village in the land, to ensure that it becomes bigger still.' *Morning Star*, 25 September 1978. The Communists are saying that it is the duty of the churches to contribute to the growth of the A.N.L. As a Christian who was present at the A.N.L. Carnival, that is a question I wish to discuss. We have a duty to uphold Christian standards of justice and mercy. We have a duty to work for love and understanding between people of different races. We also have a duty to look behind the masks of what people appear to be saying and find out what they are really saying and working towards before we give them our support. My conclusion from the A.N.L. Carnival is that it is a movement which is led and supported by people who are for the most part extremely anti-Christian and who are aiming at political goals which go far beyond mere opposition to the National Front. They may welcome the support of Christians, particularly of church leaders, who are willing to give assent to the direction the movement is taking, and thereby give it an air of respectability. However our experience shows that the overwhelming majority when actually faced with the Gospel show a strongly anti-Christian reaction.

As the march went through Brixton a small group of us were handing out leaflets about our faith in the Lord Jesus Christ. The gist of the message on the leaflet was that it is not enough to be just *against* racism, you have to be *for* something, and went on to explain why we were for Jesus. Two of our team were standing further up the march, so by the time the marchers reached me several people already had leaflets, so I was able to assess reaction to them. The overwhelming majority were contemptuous in their rejection as soon as they realized that it was about the Lord, with many statements of hatred towards his name being expressed. I was very conscious of the presence of a powerful anti-Christian force, as supporters of revolutionary Communist groups, homosexual and lesbian liberation groups and punk-rockers passed by. In the park itself Marxist and libertarian ideas were being put over to the background of rock music. Literature was being distributed and sold from causes ranging from the legalization of cannabis to support for violent terrorist groups abroad. The effect of the rock music was to create an atmosphere of mesmerization and mental blankness into which occasional doses of heavy political propaganda could be injected. It was clear to anyone with political discernment that the organizers also realized that it is not enough to be just against racism, you have to be for something. They were offering socialism of the revolutionary Marxist kind, as the cause to fight for. I was reminded of the words of Jerry Rubin, the American 'Yippie' (anarchist) leader: 'We've combined youth, music, sex, drugs and rebellion with treason – and that's a combination hard to beat.' This combination was in evidence at the A.N.L. Carnival, and it is certainly hard to beat, because it is a combination which is brought together, orchestrated and led by the powers of darkness, preparing the way for the coming Antichrist.

The National Front (N.F.) have done a great service to the revolutionary left in this country. They have provided an enemy to fight, opposition to which creates a unifying

force which is more immediate and relevant than campaigns like the Anti-Vietnam War Movement or the Anti-
Apartheid Movement which in recent years have served
as Communist front organizations. However, despite the
vociferous slogans of hatred for Webster and Tyndall
(leaders of N.F.) which were being chanted on the march,
I am convinced that the N.F. are not the real enemy the
A.N.L. leadership are aiming at. Reading between the lines
of their propaganda one realizes that they are cleverly
focusing hostility on the Capitalist system and the democratic institutions of this country. Consider this from the
handout advertising the Carnival:

> 'Black people don't cause unemployment – in the 1930s
> three million people were unemployed, when very few
> black people lived in Britain. It is not black people who
> cause 300,000 building workers or 8,000 architects to
> be unemployed. Nor 800,000 second and third homes
> belonging to the rich which stand empty. It is not black
> people that keep 20,000 trained teachers on the dole
> while classrooms are overcrowded. The Nazi N.F. do
> nothing to stop hospitals closing, nurseries and schools
> being shut down and unemployment rising. Instead they
> peddle racialist lies about black people. But it is not only
> the Nazi N.F. who do this. Thatcher's remarks about
> "black people swamping the country", recent decisions
> in the courts, the report by a committee of the House
> of Commons, all show that the racialist ideas of the Nazis
> are getting wider support.'

This kind of rhetoric is the standard propaganda of the
Socialist Workers' Party (S.W.P.), the founders and
driving force behind the A.N.L. It is very easy for a trained
Marxist to take any unsuspecting and gullible young
person on from this point into a Marxist analysis of what

is wrong with society and how to change it (For instance, 'Black people don't cause unemployment, who does? The Capitalist System.' 'Racialist ideas are gaining support in the House of Commons, politicians are racist and against the interests of the majority. If you want racial justice and freedom, it is right to rebel against the government.') On this point it is instructive to consider what the S.W.P. hold to be racialist ideas. The S.W.P. favour unlimited immigration to Britain and the abolition of immigration controls. This policy, which exists in no other country in the world, is in our present circumstances totally impractical and, if implemented, would bring chaos and a total breakdown of community relations in the country. However the S.W.P. brand anyone who opposes this policy as a racist and therefore a Fascist. By this tactic they are able to paint politicians who favour immigration controls as racists and Fascists. They then go on to equate these politicians with Hitler and the Nazis, and equate rebellion against a legally elected democratic government with resistance to the Nazis. The extent to which Margaret Thatcher's name is appearing in current A.N.L. propaganda is significant. Consider this as one of the entertainments provided at the Carnival and reported in the *Morning Star*:

'You could knock down a picture of Martin Webster, Enoch Powell, Hitler or Thatcher ... *Morning Star*, 25 August 1978.

What has Margaret Thatcher, the leader of a democratic political party which supports the rule of law, to do with Adolf Hitler, the demonically inspired leader of a party whose propaganda and actions from the outset expressed contempt for democracy and the rule of law? I believe this equation is dangerous, misleading and evil, not because I wish to canvass support for Mrs Thatcher or the Conservative Party, but because it is a deliberate piece of political manipulation by extreme left forces which are even now preparing the revolutionary forces to overthrow the government. By equating Mrs Thatcher with Hitler and the Tories with Nazis, they are able to adopt a high moral tone of campaigning for justice and freedom, when they are really aiming at a Marxist revolution and govern- ment which will be every bit as terrible as an N.F. govern- ment. In my opinion, since the Marxists are backed by a powerful international force, they are more likely to win the present struggle for power than the Fascists.[21]

The polarization of political extremes is one of the out- comes of social deprivation. In a situation of social stress, due to unemployment or low standards of housing and education or a lack of social amenities, there is a tendency for people to look to the purveyors of political extremism to provide answers to what appear to be desperate situations. There is inevitably a disenchantment with government, a feeling of helplessness and a general belief that those in authority either do not know or do not care about the plight of the poor and the disprivileged. It is under this kind of circumstance that anti-Establishment and anti-authority atti- tudes are generated, which give rise to political movements of either the far Left or the far Right. Such movements are not usually generated *from within* social stress situations. They are usually thought out by people living under quite different conditions and are introduced into the stress area from out- side. Once introduced they find ready support from those who believe themselves to be suffering from some form of social injustice.

In Britain today it is the Left who pose the greatest threat of revolution. In terms of organization and potential for political power they are often grossly underrated. Many, even amongst those closely associated with them, believe them to be lacking in efficient organization.

The apparent informality or even casualness does not, however, imply a lack of organization or commitment or dedication. Branch meetings of the I.S. are often cancelled at the last minute and this, to the outside observer, implies inefficiency in the organization, whereas in fact the reverse is true. What usually happens is that members are required for active duty somewhere in the area. If there is an industrial dispute nearby, members of the Marxist cell in that area will take it upon themselves to give active support in some way. If there is a demonstration, they will join it. If there is a picket line, they will be on it. If there is a group of workers protesting outside the headquarters of their employers, they will be among them. If there is a group of tenants or local residents lobbying councillors at the Town Hall, or lobbying members before a meeting of the Education Committee or the Housing Committee, the Marxists will join them. Their intention is to exacerbate any industrial or social situation where there is disagreement between workers and employers or between members of the public and those in authority.

The same faces turn up time and again on different picket lines and demonstrations to wave banners, to shout slogans and to distribute Marxist propaganda. Ostensibly they are supporting the under-dogs against those in authority. They are acting as champions of the oppressed. But in reality their purpose is to increase discontent with management amongst workers, or among members of the public against those in authority. The more they can widen the gap in a dispute, the longer they can prolong arrival at a settlement and the more they can gather support for the dispute by widening its basis, spreading it to other industrial plants or gaining the support of workers in allied industries, the more they are achieving their purpose. That purpose is to inflict greater and greater damage to the economy, until it either collapses or it is so weak that a political revolution could succeed.

The purpose of the Marxists is to create more and more discontent amongst workers, widening the gap between the shop floor and management in every section of industry, stirring up class hatred as part of the struggle against capitalism, with the ultimate objective of mobilizing the working classes to the point where the ultimate challenge to authority and government can be successful. Their clear intention is to *destroy democracy, not to reform it*!

Despite the confusion of the present situation, in which political extremes have been polarized and there appears to be an equal challenge from the Right and from the Left, the real threat to the future of democracy in Britain is from the Left. The Right are dangerous, but they are dangerous only in terms of side effect. The right-wing extremists give the opportunity to the Left to pose as the defenders of democracy. The Marxists are able to warn that there will be no freedom under the jack-boots of the fascists if the N.F. ever come to power. In this, of course, they are perfectly right, as recent European history has amply demonstrated. Nevertheless, there is great danger that under the cloak of 'defenders of freedom' the Left will gain power.

The very fact that so many well intentioned idealists are willing to share the same platform, and to join with Marxists in demonstrations and other political activities, is an indication of the aura of respectability they have now gained. The Lewisham demonstration, that ended with some of the most violent scenes ever witnessed in London, began with a communion service led by the Bishop of Southwark. After the service, when the Christians took to the streets they were joined by a hotchpotch of individuals and organizations representing everything from homosexuals to Marxists. It was then that events overtook them. The Christians lost control of the demonstration, and what began as a peaceful protest against the evils of racism ended in blood, destruction and mindless violence.

Many deeply religious people, others with a strong social conscience, and those with genuine social grievances suffering from exploitation, injustice and racism, have a very real concern to fight for social justice and to work unceasingly for basic changes in the structure of our society. But the battle for social justice should not be confused with the war that the Marxists are waging. The end products of the two are totally different.

The idealists (many of whom are deeply committed Christians) are seeking a new basis of society in which there will be full freedom for every individual to live, to work and to worship in a caring, sharing society. The Marxists, by contrast, seek only to replace one form of oppression with another.

The great danger today is that the idealists are being used by Marxists. Issues become blurred, ultimate objectives obscured. Many of the idealists are only too glad to have the help of anyone who will assist in drawing attention to the terrible social injustices that exist amongst the less privileged people who live in our inner-city areas. Unfortunately they do not realize that they are being used.

The day will surely come, when the economy has been sufficiently weakened and anti-authority attitudes have been sufficiently exacerbated, when the Left will mount a massive demonstration on some social issue supported by vast numbers of idealists and fellow travellers. The demonstration may begin in Hyde Park and sweep through the streets of London, but it will not stop at Trafalgar Square! It will go on down Whitehall to capture the seat of power.

The Revolution will be on!

SPIRITUAL FACTORS

Where there is no redemptive revelation of
God the people perish.
                    Proverbs 29:18
                    (Amplified Version)

CHAPTER FIVE

SPIRITUAL FACTORS

We have seen in the previous two chapters something of the way in which the destructive forces are at work in our society today. There is the growing confusion in the political scene, with the increasing polarization of political forces into Left and Right and a strong movement towards the extremes on both wings of the political chicken. There is also strong evidence that the forces of social change are gathering momentum to the point where the whole structure of organized social life in Britain is likely to be swept away.

The forces of social change at work in the country today that are tearing down one tradition after another are, in fact, aiding the political extremists, who are convinced that a revolution is the only means of attaining their goals. The withering of social organization, the weakening of social norms, and a general air of chaos and confusion in society can only aid the ambitions of revolutionaries. These are the very conditions under which a political revolution could be successful. It is very much easier to challenge the legitimate forces of law and order in a society where there is a lack of well-regulated social life. These are the conditions under which revolutionaries are able to pose as social saviours – the restorers of law and order – the preservers of the tradi- tional heritage – the true patriots – the only ones able to restore the country's fortunes and to bring back the former glories. Hitler, Mussolini and Franco each came to power in Europe under similar circumstances, and in the Third World in recent years we have seen numerous examples of fascist dictators gaining power in conditions of social chaos

It was for this reason that we said in chapter 4 that a revolution in Britain could emanate either from the Left or from the Right, although concluding that the most significant challenge in terms of organization and resources is coming from the Left.

If this analysis is correct it is therefore clear that we have two distinct movements, one of which is political and economic while the other is social and moral (or normative). Both of these movements, while they can be distinguished for analytical purposes, are in fact strongly interrelated and are moving towards a point of convergence. It is impossible at this stage to forecast which will reach the point of climax first. It is also quite possible that they may both climax at the same point for, as we have just noted, conditions of social disorientation are ideal for those who are planning revolution. We should not conclude from this that a revolutionary threat is more likely to come from the Right under these conditions.

The weakening of the social and normative structures of society inevitably affects the economy, and as the economy is brought to the point of breakdown through violent industrial action by the workers, a successful challenge to government from the Left could well be undertaken.

If we were pressed for the most likely outcome of the two political revolutionary alternatives that are mounting in Britain today, this would appear to be the more likely.

There is, however, a third force at work in Britain today of which we need to take careful account before coming to any clear prognostications. It is the power of the Holy Spirit.

Renewal Movement

Christians who are conversant with the national scene and who are able to discern the signs of the times believe that there is unmistakable evidence of a new movement of the Holy Spirit in Britain today.[22] The charismatic renewal movement which began in the mid-1960s was the first real indication of this movement. Like all new movements it had its scenes of exuberant excesses, but there is solid evidence to suggest that the excesses of the early days are now a thing of the past and that what we are seeing is real spiritual renewal in the life of a great many churches. The renewal movement has brought a new joy, openness and spontaneity in worship that were missing in the vast majority of churches in Britain. Worship had become dull, traditional and stereotyped, and through the renewal movement many churches throughout the country have experienced new life – a real coming alive in the Lord. Churches that previously had no Biblical tradition have found through the renewal movement a new interest in the scriptures, a new desire to study them eagerly and to accept them as the authoritative word of God. Prayer and Bible study are the roots of revival, and this is precisely what we are seeing in church after church of different denominations and different traditions throughout the country. There is a new interest in spiritual growth and a new emphasis upon koinonia-type fellowship in the Lord.

One of the cornerstones of the new movement is the emphasis upon small groups where ordinary Christians are getting together to study the scriptures, to pray and to share their faith with each other. This simple act of faith-sharing is giving a new confidence to Christians to discuss their faith in a way that they had previously never done. Many Christians in Britain were brought up with the idea that religion and politics were taboo in polite society. It was simply not done to talk about the 'deep things' of the soul. Small group fellowships give ordinary Christians the confidence to speak about their faith and their experience of Christ. Previously they were not only given no opportunity to speak about their faith, but were actually positively discouraged from doing so by the strictly patterned acts of public worship that they were expected to attend more as observers than participants; where only the ordained minister or priest led the worship or spoke about spiritual things. This inevitably gave the impression that you had to be a professional Christian in order to speak about your faith.

The renewal movement has blown all that apart. It has given to ordinary Christians the opportunity to be witnesses to their faith in the same way as New Testament Christians were. Not everyone can be an evangelist but everyone can be a witness. A witness is simply someone who has had a personal experience. Christians who have had a personal experience of Jesus and who have allowed him to be Lord in their lives have been learning in small groups how to speak quite simply of their innermost spiritual experiences, and have thus gained the confidence to be able to share their faith with their non-Christian neighbours. The renewal movement has laid the foundations for a new type of evangelism – at least, new to a great many of the traditional churches in Britain – that of personal evangelism and faith-sharing on a one-to-one basis. It is primarily a movement led by ordinary Christians with no theological training and not by professional evangelists.

A further indication of the new spiritual movement is the proliferation of para-church organizations. With any new spiritual movement there is a tendency for fission and fusion to take place in the early days, when there is a strong emphasis upon the experiential basis of belief. Members of groups who have had a similar type of spiritual experience have believed this to be of paramount importance in meeting together to share what they have in common. The growth of the independent house fellowship movement is one of the inevitable consequences of spiritual renewal. Whenever a new movement breaks into a highly traditional situation it is like putting new wine into old wine skins. Sometimes the old skins burst because they cannot retain the amount of activity that is going on inside. Many traditional churches have experienced considerable tensions within the membership due to some members having had a new spiritual experience and others not. Those who have not resist the new emphasis, or teaching, or type of worship that is being advocated by a minority group and which threatens to undermine the cherished traditions held for many years. If the power in the church is held by the traditionalists, then it is those who advocate change who move out and either establish a new church or simply link up in a house fellowship. Today there is an unknown number (certainly in the thousands) of house fellowships of varying size up and down the country, some of whom are linked in groups of fellowships and others of whom are entirely independent.

The charismatic movement is no respecter of denomination or tradition. One of the remarkable and perhaps exciting new dimensions in the renewal movement is that it is sweeping aside denominational boundaries, and linking Christians who formerly had nothing to do with each other. It sometimes brings into living and vital fellowship those who formerly did not even recognize each other as Christian. Many Roman Catholics have been baptized in the spirit in recent years ar.d have been discovering a Biblical basis to faith such as they had not previously known. Many Christians from the Reformed churches and from evangelical traditions have been finding themselves entering into fellowship in Christ with Roman Catholics. This is something that before the renewal movement would have been totally unthinkable for them. This blurring of distinctions is something that some

Christians find extremely puzzling. It is reminiscent of the experience of the Jews in the early Church when heated discussions took place leading up to the Council of Jerusalem (Acts 15), where the Gentiles were for the first time officially admitted into the fellowship of the Body of Christ. Countless times the Jewish Christians exclaimed amongst themselves, 'The Gentiles have received the Holy Spirit in the same way as we ourselves have!' (see Acts 10:45 and 15:8).

One of the genuine marks of a new spiritual movement is that God does an entirely new thing, unforeseen and unexpected by those who have held a traditional religious belief.

This is a day of new revelation when God is beginning to create all things new, when we are having to learn new ways and having to adjust to new spiritual insights. Inevitably there are tensions and misunderstandings. There are those who resist changes because they dislike any form of change. There are others who take a delight in anything new, embracing it with a joyous certainty and simplicity of belief that it is of the Lord, while there are others again who are more cautious by nature and wish to test anything new to ensure that it is of the Spirit before giving it wholehearted commitment. Tensions, therefore, inevitably arise but they are a mark of growth, like growing pains in the body, and should be regarded as healthy and creative rather than feared as indications of disunity.

Some Christians mistakenly regard unity as something to be prized above all things, whereas a time of new revelation inevitably produces some division. In fact, a lack of any disagreement may sometimes be a sign of complacency and decay, whereas the presence of tension within the Christian Church may be a sign of a new creative movement of the Holy Spirit – resisted by the traditionalists and embraced gladly by those who are open to the Lord and expecting him to do a new thing in their day. Having said this we have, at the same time, to recognize the dangers to unity of such a time as this, when traditions are being shattered, new practices introduced and new structures evolving.

This is not unique in the history of the Church. Before the close of the New Testament, Christians were having to face the problems of revealed truth versus established tradition. John warned his young converts not to believe all the spirits, 'but test the spirits to see whether they are of God; for many false prophets have gone out into the world' (1 John 4:1). The simple test that John recommended was a confession of faith in Jesus as Messiah.

The situation facing us today is fundamentally different from that existing in the first century AD. In those days it was rationalists who were challenging the Lordship of Jesus, in both traditional and experiential belief. Today the challenge is coming from an opposite polarity. It is the rationalists, who have dominated the major protestant denominations throughout this century, who are now being challenged by the experiential belief of those who have come alive in Christ through the ministry of the Holy Spirit. The real danger arises when these spiritually alive Christians lack a sound doctrinal basis rooted in Biblical tradition.

It is precisely this situation that is creating division within the Body of Christ. Numerous examples could be quoted of groups within the house-church movement where the leadership exercised is that of an authoritarianism vested in an individual, whose word is the decisive ruling in all matters of belief and practice. A similar situation exists in a number of established churches, such as those where the tradition has been one of liberal theology and liturgical worship. The writer personally knows of charismatic Anglo-Catholic vicars who offer courses of instruction in the use of the rosary for charismatics, who mix Hail Marys, incense and tongues in public worship, and who when challenged on a point of doctrine or practice give the unanswerable reply that the Holy Spirit has told them. A similar situation exists in liberal churches of non-liturgical traditions where there has been an outpouring of the Holy Spirit resulting in the exercise of spiritual gifts not rooted in Biblical tradition. This has often resulted in factions within the church and a kind of spiritual one-upmanship between rival factions.

It is a pointless exercise merely to catalogue 'hairy stories' from what some would regard as the lunatic fringe of the charismatic movement. We are here simply stating the fact that the movement has within it a very wide spectrum of belief and practice. In the writer's view this underlines the need for a sound basis of Biblical authority in any new spiritual movement. We are not pleading for a blind literalism, but for a scholarly approach to the Bible that combines an experience of the presence and power of the risen Christ with an eager searching of scripture to discover the authoritative word of God which meets the needs of modern man both in our present generation and in facing the great issues confronting us in this age.

Youth and Renewal

A further indication of a new movement of the Holy Spirit is to be seen amongst young people in Britain. Thousands of them have been accepting the Gospel and turning to Christ in recent years. There is throughout the country, amongst young people from all types of background, a new openness to Christianity and an eagerness to search for spiritual truth Amongst students this new spiritual movement is clearly discernible. In most universities and colleges in Britain today the largest student organizations are Christian, whereas a few years ago they were political. It is not uncommon today for there to be hundreds of students attending meetings organized by the Christian Union, whereas only a handful go to the Marxist group or meetings organized by other political bodies. Freedom in praise and a joyful spontaneity in worship, plus a new interest in discovering a Biblical basis as the foundation to life, are the major characteristics of the student gatherings. They are clearly discernible as the hall-mark of a new movement of the Holy Spirit amongst young people.

There can be no doubt that part of the motivation of the spiritual search of many young people is disillusionment. It is a hatred of the injustices and anomalies of life, the excesses of luxury enjoyed by a small minority and the grinding poverty endured by vast numbers of the world's under-privileged peoples. They have been brought up in a world where two-thirds of its population suffer from hunger and privation and one person dies of starvation every five seconds, and where in the remaining one-third who enjoy a high standard of living, the wealth of the capitalist nations is controlled by less than two per cent of their populations.

Many young people grow up with the feeling of disillusion-ment and alienation from society – a disillusionment with the politicians, leaders and Establishment figures who to them appear to lack integrity, to be content with the *status quo* because it gives them high status and privilege, and to be unconcerned with the underprivileged. Young people feel powerless and unable to influence the course of events. They feel caught up in the processes at work in society that they believe to be unjust and evil, and they see 'the Establish-ment' – political, social and religious – as contriving to support an unjust social order and allowing the forces of darkness to continue unabated in the life of our nation.

It is due to this disillusionment and lack of confidence in the leaders of the nation that many young people are turning away from politics and social philosophy, and are looking for spiritual answers to the pernicious problems of our age. Equally they reject the traditional religion of their elders, and look directly to scripture for the revelation of God's truth, his word for his world, and to their own experience of the Holy Spirit for confirmation of the truth they read in scripture. Thus it is hardly surprising that the new movement of the Spirit amongst young people is characterized by a new freedom in worship and the use of a wide range of Christian music often resembling the fashions of the pop world.

New Opportunity

The new openness to the Gospel we have just noted amongst young people is not, however, confined to the younger generation. We were noting in an earlier chapter the evidence of economic and social malaise in the life of the nation. We are living in days of enormous tension and social stress, where the evidence of moral and spiritual decay is clearly discernible even to the non-religious and to those who claim to care for none of these things. The economic instability of the nation and chronic inflation have a demoralizing effect upon everyone.

The incessant upward spiral of one price rise after another, plus the unending demand for wage and salary increases and for bigger profits and dividends, seem to continue with sickening monotony. The ever-increasing tensions between workers and management in industry, plus the sparring of the big union bosses, the economic strangle-hold of big monopolies, the blackmail exercised by the OPEC countries with the continuing oil crisis, all add to the sense of powerlessness experienced by most ordinary citizens today. Then there is the violence in our cities, the challenge to law and order on our streets, the pollution of pornography in our newspaper shops, and the presence of vice and moral corruption at every level in society. There are also the personal problems that so many ordinary people suffer from today, the depressions caused by strains and breakdowns in personal relationships. There is the vast increase of family and marriage breakdown, with all the consequent suffering and nervous strains and tensions inflicted upon the young and innocent as well as upon the guilty. Ours is a sick society and what's more, we know it! The vast majority of ordinary people know that there is something wrong with the life of the nation in Britain today.

It is a fact of the utmost significance that it is not simply Christians and traditional moralists who recognize that Britain is sick. There is an uneasy feeling throughout the nation that something is very fundamentally wrong with Britain today. The series of industrial strikes in the early months of 1979, that shook the economy deeply enough to bring about the downfall of the Labour Government, caused widespread concern throughout the country. In the subsequent General Election the nation gave the Tories a majority without any overwhelming enthusiasm – almost a dull sense of resignation that any change could only be for the better! Even in the euphoria of the post-election honeymoon there was no general confidence that Britain now had a group of politicians in government who would answer all the nation's problems. Indeed the Thatcher government made post-war history in the first three months of its life by its landslide fall from grace in the eyes of the nation, as its popularity ratings slumped in the opinion polls. Never was Bernard Shaw's cynical political observation more apt than in the midsummer of 1979. Shaw likened the change of government at a General Election to the turning over of the muck heap in the farmyard – it simply brings a different lot of maggots to the top! Within a few weeks most people in Britain had realized that a change of government would solve nothing. We had simply exchanged one lot of sinners for another. It was still the same old nation. The general anxiety remained.

It is this widespread unease and anxiety that is of the greatest significance for the future of evangelism in Britain. Already there is strong evidence to suggest that the tide of unbelief has turned. There is a new openness to the Gospel amongst the ordinary people in Britain today, such as there has not been throughout the years of this century. People are search-ing for a new basis of life for the nation, and they are searching too for answers to their own personal problems. There is a new hunger for truth, a new openness to spiritual things, and a new opportunity for the proclamation of the Gospel such as has not been known in the lifetime of most Christians. There is a deep longing, amongst millions of people who have no knowledge of the Gospel, for authorita-tive answers to the multitude of personal and national problems that beset us. People do not want half-hearted vague opinions, they want authoritative answers that really work.

This new openness to the Gospel is to be found amongst all ages and all sections of the population. Recently a group of churches in a tough docklands area of the East End of London got together for a united evangelistic outreach. (That in itself is quite a remarkable happening! Although they were all from Bible-believing churches they represented very different traditions, pentecostal and non-pentecostal, including some Christians who hadn't even spoken to each other for twenty-five years. Surely evidence of the work of the Holy Spirit!) Part of the outreach was outdoor meetings in the market and in the park, but an important part was a house-to-house visitation. A great deal of research, planning and prayer went into this part of the combined mission. Each church had to find out all it could about the families in the streets in its neighbourhood. Then at united prayer meetings they were prayed for house by house, before ever a single door was knocked on. When finally the visitors went out two by two, supported by prayer teams back at base, there was a real air of quiet purposive confidence amongst all those taking part. The really remarkable thing about the two-month visitation campaign in the area was that there was not a single report of a door being shut in a visitor's face. Five years ago, even two years ago, this would have been impossible. East-Enders have for years been sick to death of religion and the Church, of missions and the 'Establishment' and all that goes with it. There has been a massive rejection of institutional Christianity by the vast majority of the population. Barely one per cent attend church today in the East End of London. Sixty per cent of all the churches and missions have closed during the past twenty-five years. Even the Salvation Army has virtually been annihilated from the East End, where it began a hundred years ago. Going from the City of London east into Essex there is only one corps of the Salvation Army left, and that has only a handful of soldiers remaining under the leadership of a woman Lieutenant.

It is a truly remarkable thing that in one of the toughest areas in the East End of London, traditionally amongst the most difficult areas for the Gospel in Britain, amongst hundreds of houses contacted not a single door was slammed in the face of Christian visitors. In fact there were some quite remarkable stories of residents throwing wide the doors when they realized they had Christian visitors and inviting them in to talk. In family after family there were found to be anxieties and personal problems that people were longing to talk over with someone. There is a new opportunity for the Gospel now amongst ordinary people of all ages and all sectors of the population. In theological terms, it is almost as if the devil has over-reached himself, and the sickness and decay of our society are having a backlash effect that is creating a hunger for the Gospel.

There is thus evidence of two things happening at the same time. In the first place, there is clear evidence of a new movement of the Holy Spirit, a new spiritual awakening amongst Christians and new dimensions of worship, fellowship and evangelism. Secondly, there is equally clear evidence of a new openness to the Gospel amongst ordinary men, women and young people throughout the country. The anxiety over personal and national problems is creating a hunger for authoritative answers and an openness to spiritual truth. If we put these two factors together they add up to the creation of a time of immense opportunity for evangelism in Britain. For those who have eyes to see and ears to hear, God is opening up the avenues of spiritual communication with the ordinary people of this land, in a way that we have not experienced for many decades. Those who have the most sensitive fingers on the pulse of the spiritual arteries of the nation believe that the 1980s will witness the greatest revival we have seen this century.

The Third Way

The major question facing us is whether the spiritual revival, which at the moment appears as a small cloud on the horizon, will come into full reality in time to save Britain from either the horrors of bloody revolution or the chaos and confusion of social disintegration.

We thus have not two alternatives as we posed at the end of the last chapter, but a choice of three things.

Which will happen first, political revolution, social collapse or spiritual revival?

There are on the religious scene several other factors of which we need to take account before we are in a position to give an answer to this question.

The major question in assessing the speed at which the new spiritual movement is likely to travel is how the churches are likely to respond to the great opportunity that is now being presented to them. Are they able to seize this new opportunity for proclaiming the Gospel to a sick nation? Are they able to transmit new life and spiritual power into a sick society? The answer surely lies in the state of the churches themselves.

While we have faithfully recorded, earlier in this chapter, evidence of a new movement of the Holy Spirit which has already resulted in many churches becoming spiritually alive, we have to recognize that we are talking about only a small proportion of the total number of churches in Britain. The vast majority of churches are stuck fast in their traditions, that may have been highly relevant and fruitful in a bygone age but are totally irrelevant and unproductive in this present generation.

Tradition is a good thing when it acts as the agent for passing on the truth from one generation to the next, but it is a shackle that imprisons the truth when it becomes inflexible and unresponsive to the changing conditions and changing needs of a new generation.

The church that refuses to consider the possibility of any change is not open to the Lord. It does not expect God to create anything new.

There is a church in the little Gloucestershire town of Northleach. Like most of the buildings in the town, it is built of solid Cotswold stone. No doubt there was a time when the little church in the centre of the town (which is on the A40 trunk road), right opposite the market square, was filled with people and radiated the presence and the glory of the

Lord. Today it is closed. The casual passer-by may wonder why. But if you stand in the market square across the street and look at the church there is a clue to the reasons for its closure. Right across the front of the building, cut deep into the Cotswold stone, are the words SUNDAY SERVICES 11 A.M. AND 6 P.M. Clearly they didn't expect anything ever to change! They never even considered it a possibility that the day might come when there would be a need to vary the times of the Sunday services to meet the changing needs of a later generation. Today that church stands empty and deserted, the weeds grow in profusion across its front door. It stands, a silent memorial to the inflexibility of tradition that gradually sapped the life from the church and inevitably brought about its death.

The church that is stuck fast in dead traditions is totally unable to radiate the presence of the living Christ. It has become a mere *human organization* and is no longer a *spiritual organism* – a living fellowship of believers alive in Christ.

A major reason why churches become inflexible and un-responsive to change is *spiritual insecurity*. The Christian life is no longer an adventure, a joyous venture of faith, but a dour clinging to tradition, a joyless determination to main-tain the *status quo*. The members of dead traditional churches are unable to face changes because they lack faith. They are lacking in faith because they lack trust in the Lord. They are lacking in trust because they lack vision. Scripture rightly says 'Where there is no vision the people perish' (Proverbs 29:18; A.V.). *Vision derives from the word of the Lord*, and so too does the power of the Holy Spirit. We need the Spirit to bring the word to life. When we are open to the Lord and accept the authority of His word two things happen – we catch a vision of the kingdom and we receive the power of the Spirit. We then come under the controlling guidance of the Lord and we are given the power to transform the vision into a living reality. That openness to the Lord is missing in many of our churches. It is missing due to the deadening effects of the process of institutionalization through which the life and vitality that were experienced in Christian fellowships in bygone generations have gradually become routinized and fixed and part of an unalterable tradition.

The seven last words of a dying church are, 'We have always done it this way'! When we are wedded to tradition we are stuck fast in a groove, and the only difference between a groove and a grave is one of depth! A blind adherence to traditionalism, whether it be found amongst Bible-believing churches or those of liberal theological traditions, is equally deadening. If a church is stuck fast in tradition it is unable to respond to the changing circumstances and needs of a new generation, and it tends simply to play out the time-honoured role, with everybody doing everything just as they used to and as their fathers did before them, without heed to the actual effectiveness of what they are doing. The church ceases to grow. It becomes inward-looking and defensive. The members no longer expect new people to come and join them, and the preachers reflect this insularity in their messages, which become adapted to the needs of the faithful few. They even justify theologically their small numbers and lack of growth – there's nothing more popular today amongst preachers of little congregations than remnant theology!

The church that is not growing is dead! This is the unpalatable truth that thousands of churches refuse to face. The basic property of all living matter is growth! Without growth there is no life, without life we are dead. Churches that are not growing numerically are often spiritually dead, because numerical growth is one of the signs of, and usually a result of, spiritual growth. Where a fellowship is alive in Christ and growing spiritually, its members are keen and active and cannot help sharing their faith with their non-Christian friends. Their witness inevitably bears fruit, they take their neighbours with them to church or to their house fellowship, and the fellowship grows numerically. An over-concern with tradition results in a lack of expectancy of anything new. Once we cease to expect the Lord, the God of creation, the Alpha and Omega, to create anything new, we are closed to the Spirit. Churches of both liberal and evangelical traditions can be closed to the Spirit, but that closure may stem from different roots and show itself in different ways.

In order rightly to assess the situation in the country we need to look separately at churches of the 'liberal' and 'evangelical' traditions.

THE LIBERALS

In a great many churches of the major denominations there is today a spiritual barrenness in the life of the fellowship, due to the fact that the congregation rarely, if ever, hears the authentic word of God. The theological basis of the Reformation, from which all protestant churches have sprung, was its emphasis upon the centrality of the word of God. This was even symbolized in the design and building of Non-Conformist churches. In most of the older Free Churches the pulpit occupied the central position at the front of the church, and immediately in front of it stood the communion table with an open Bible facing the people. This symbolized the central importance of the word of God, open to the people and expounded from the pulpit. It is the word of God that provides us with our basic faith and with our

hope of salvation in Christ, the ordering of church government and the pattern of our life style, both as a Christian
community and as individual members of the Body of Christ.
Without the word of God in scripture we have no authoritative basis for our faith. That is why many churches were
built to emphasize the central importance of the scriptures,
and why all the worshippers brought their own copy of the
Bible so that they could follow the exposition of the word
from the pulpit which it was the preacher's prime task to
deliver. In most modern churches of the Reformed tradition,
the pulpit has now been discreetly moved to the side, the
communion table has been pushed back further away from
the people, the open Bible has disappeared, and hardly any
worshippers bother to bring Bibles to church with them.

Personal Testimony

I want to be very personal now and I trust the reader will
forgive me if for the next few pages I speak very frankly out of
my own experience. For the year 1976–7 I was national
President of my denomination, and both during that year and
subsequently I have travelled up and down the country,
preaching and speaking in a great many churches. I have been
amazed at the small importance attached to the Bible in most
of them. Hardly anyone brings a Bible to church, and consequently hardly anyone follows the reading of scripture. In
most of the churches I've visited, the order of service allows
for only one reading. The hymn book is obviously of more
importance than the Bible: we provide a copy for every
worshipper, but we don't give them a Bible as well.

But what do we hear from the pulpit? Is the word of God
faithfully expounded in most churches? I had a Sunday free
recently and went to worship in a church near my home.
The preacher was an ordained Baptist minister who is now

a college lecturer. He took his text from the Sunday news-paper *The Observer*, from a story about a Russian Jewish dissident psychiatrist who had said, 'You have to recognize that you are a human being and behave like one at some time in your life.' There was no scriptural basis to the sermon at all. It was full of little stories about people being good human beings, and about hunger in the Third World and the need for social justice. It ended with these words, and I quote: 'Being saved in the sense of making us fit for heaven is irrelevant; we can leave that to God. What matters is becoming truly human.' In the end the preacher had revealed himself for what he really is – a *humanist*! For me, the saddest thing was to hear people around me saying how good it was. They had been entertained with some nice little stories that had been pleasantly put together and well presented, so they believed that they had heard a good sermon. But there was no Gospel in it! The preacher had told us how to be a good human being, not how to come into a living relationship with God, through Christ.

In Ezekiel chapter 34 there is a terrible picture of the shepherds of Israel failing to feed and care for their sheep. For this reason the sheep were scattered 'because there was no shepherd and they became food for all the wild beasts' (34:5). God then pronounced judgement upon the unfaithful shepherds: 'My shepherds have not searched for my sheep, but the shepherds have fed themselves, and have not fed my sheep ... Behold, I am against the shepherds; and I will require my sheep at their hand' (34:8–10).

The judgement that Ezekiel pronounces upon the religious leaders of Israel who have misled the people, applies strikingly to our own situation today. We have a whole generation of ministers who are suffering from an overdose of Biblical criticism and liberal theology taught in a sterile, academic framework. I can speak with considerable authority here because this is precisely the tradition in which I was educated.

I went into theological college a simple Bible-believing Christian, under the firm conviction that the Lord had called me to be a preacher. It wasn't long, however, before the Bible was systematically torn apart for me, and the whole basis of my faith shattered. I'm not complaining about the scholarship I was taught. I believe it is right that men in training for the ministry should have the best theological education available to them, and that includes the fruits of the critical scholarship concerning authorship and textual problems now available to us. It is the *context* in which this teaching takes place that is all important. When Biblical studies are taught by men with no personal experience of Christ and without a basis of faith in their own lives, then their teaching becomes nothing more than a barren negativistic academic exercise.

I, like thousands of other ministers over the past generation or so, left college with a good classical and theological education, but with no real living faith in God. Such faith as I once had having been systematically destroyed. Consequently, I lacked the power of the Holy Spirit in the early part of my ministry. It was not until some years later, when I came alive in Christ, that I rediscovered the Bible and it became precious to me as the word of God. Although I certainly did not react into a blind literalist view of scripture, my faith no longer depended upon the outcome of critical debate. I discovered a new basis of faith in my experience of the presence of the risen Lord in my life. It was from this certainty in Christ that I was able to come back and wrestle with the thorniest problems of Biblical criticism, without disturbing my peace in God. I have experienced the power of the Holy Spirit which has brought a new spiritual dimension, a new joy and peace into my life that was certainly not there before. I not only know that there is a difference in my own personal life, but that there is a difference in my ministry too. In the earlier years of my ministry I never saw

anyone converted, and I didn't know what it meant to be
alive in Christ, but since I have come alive myself I have
seen the fruits in my ministry. I have seen people converted
and I have seen many nominal and traditional Christians
come alive in Christ in the same way that I have done.

In making this personal testimony I am aware that many
of my brother ministers will think that I am being judge-
mental on them and their ministries. I want to deny this
emphatically. I have no right to judge their ministries and
I have no wish to do so. But this is my dilemma: I can't
keep quiet about what has happened to me! I have had a
new experience of Christ and I now feel and see the power
of the Holy Spirit at work in my own life. If I did not
speak of these things I should be denying the reality of God
in my life, denying the message he has given me to declare,
and denying the mission he has given me to accomplish. At
the same time I understand the men who have not had the
same experience as I have had. I know how I used to feel
when I heard someone claiming a spiritual experience which
I didn't possess. I also know of their sincerity and integrity.

There are thousands of ministers in all the major denominations today who have been brought up in the tradition
of liberal Biblical theology, who have sincere and honest
doubts about the most basic tenets of the Christian faith. I
spent a few hours recently with a bishop in the Church of
England who doesn't believe in the Resurrection. It is not unknown even for the principal of a theological college to deny
the divinity of Christ. Yet such a man is training theological
students for the ministry of one of the major denominations.
I often speak to ministers who admit that they have no faith
and don't know what they really believe, but who are caught
in the trap of the ministry. They have no qualifications to
do any other job. They couldn't afford to buy a house for
their family with today's inflated prices, so they are trapped
in the ministry and simply play out the traditional role that's

expected of them with no enthusiasm and, of course, with no spiritual power.

Many ministers stay in the ministry because they feel they have a genuine task in caring for people. They do not speak about their doubts in public, as they have no wish to disturb the faith of the faithful. They believe that God has called them to be pastors and shepherds, and to the best of their ability they faithfully carry out this task.

I am aware that I am now in great danger of generalizing and being misunderstood. I am *not* saying that all ministers are like this! But the fact is that *some* are. And a great many more are dull and lifeless in their ministry because they lack the centrality of the word of God, a personal experience of the living Christ and the dynamic power of the Holy Spirit in their lives. If a man lacks the driving force of an inner certainty of the presence of the living Christ within him, he cannot be open to the power of the Holy Spirit in his ministry. The ministry then becomes simply another job that a man carries out in his own strength and using his own insights and abilities. He may be good with people, he may be a good listener or a good counsellor and so he's known as a good pastor, but worship becomes dull and routine, and the life of the fellowship withers. There's no enthusiasm, no excitement of greeting new people every week, no sense of real purpose and direction.

I was speaking recently at a public meeting organized by the Council of Churches in a Midlands city, and sharing something of my vision of the dangers facing the nation and of the challenge to Christians. I also spoke of my hope for a time of real growth and spiritual renewal, both in the churches and in the life of the nation. One minister got to his feet during question time and disagreed with just about everything I had said. He ended with a plea to me not to say that the churches are dead, because that simply makes things much more difficult for the ministers. 'Things are difficult enough as it is,' he said. 'The ministry is a slog. It is a hard slog and we have to just keep on faithfully slogging away at it. There is no other way.' I felt incredibly sorry for this man and I understood what he meant. He was an older man, with just a year or two to go before retirement. He had had a long ministry during what must surely be the leanest period for the Christian Church in Britain for centuries. He had seen congregations dwindle over the years, and he is now facing retirement without hope, without joy and without any real sense of satisfaction.

Clearly there is something radically wrong when the ministry is a 'slog'. It's an indication that we're doing it in our own strength and not being carried by the power of the Holy Spirit. There is nothing routine or dull and lifeless about the ministry. If you live in the presence of the Lord then there is something new every day, and you cannot help radiating that presence and power of the Lord that is living within you. When the minister is alive in Christ the fellowship around him becomes alive, and when it is alive and growing spiritually it must grow numerically. There is an attractive power about the presence of Jesus. When we set him free in our lives from the shackles of tradition and live in daily expectation of him doing something new, we are carried along by the power of his Spirit.

Power of the Holy Spirit

It is this power of the Spirit that is missing in so many churches and so many ministries. There are thousands of churches in Britain today that are characterized by 'nominality'. They have for years been content to drift on in their dead traditions, with the usual weekly routine of a little comfortable, complacent pseudo-Christianity that enables them to jog along doing the same old thing in the same old way. They never experience the real thing, the living presence of the risen Christ, that blows with irresistible power through our individual lives and through our churches when we dare to open up to him.

The Greek word for power is *dunamis*, from which we get our word 'dynamite'. It was *the power of the Holy Spirit* that drove the Apostles on to the streets of Jerusalem on the day of Pentecost, to proclaim the Gospel with such irresistible power and conviction that three thousand people gave their lives to Christ on that day. Ministers and members of many churches appear to be unaware that this same power is available to us today, and that it can be seen again at work in the lives of our churches and in the life of this nation when we are prepared to take that simple act of trust and faith – taking Christ at his own word, relying on his promise to be with us always and to give us the power of his Spirit.

One of the fascinating things happening today is that many members in the nominal churches are well aware of the sickness of the nation, and are sensing that this is a day of great opportunity for the Christian churches. There is, amongst ordinary members of the major denominations, considerable frustration that the churches are not getting on with the task of evangelism with more enthusiasm and effectiveness. There is, in fact, a considerable amount of evangelistic activity throughout Britain at this present time, with numerous evangelists touring the towns and cities conducting one-, two- or three-week missions. Usually these are only supported by a minority of the churches, from evangelical traditions. In some areas, however, some of the liberal churches have been involved in fairly low-key evangelistic outreaches or 'festivals of faith', in which they can unite on a broad basis. In one West Country town a week of mission of this kind was held, but when the liberal churches decided to give it their support, most of the evangelicals withdrew. This not only weakened the unity of the outreach, but meant that very few Christians from Bible-believing traditions were available to act as counsellors to those who committed their lives to Christ during the week. A lot of pressure was put on the ministers to act as counsellors, but very few volunteered. This was discussed in the ministers' fraternal, and although some of them made excuses, others were honest enough to admit that they simply did not know what to do, that they had never seen anyone converted, and had no experience of bringing someone through a conversion experience to a full commitment to Christ.

Most church members do not know how nervous many ministers are when confronted with such situations. This is very largely due to the way in which ministers are trained. I myself was never taught how to bring anyone to Christ – in fact it was never even mentioned throughout my four years in theological college! I was stuffed full of Greek and Hebrew and Biblical criticism, of Church history, of dogma and patristics. I excelled in philosophy and sociology, but I had no idea how to bring anyone to Christ! I was never taught. It was something no one ever even talked about. It was not on the college curriculum and it never occurred to me that this was part of the job for which I was supposedly being trained.

In the liberal tradition of Christianity which has prevailed in the major denominations in Britain for the past fifty years no one *expected* anyone to be converted. It was assumed that England was a Christian country, that the right policy for our churches was to concentrate on Christian education for the young, and that from childhood people would simply grow up to be Christians.

Hence the major denominations have produced a generation of second-generation Christians with no first-generation experience!

It is small wonder that West Indian Christians in Britain,

having tried the English churches and found them wanting in faith and the power of the Holy Spirit, have founded their own churches and wryly speak of the English churches as 'the nominal churches'.

Second-generation Christians without a first-generation experience have a second-hand faith. They will tell you about their mother who was a Sunday School teacher, or their grandfather who was a lay preacher, but they are unable to speak of their own *personal* faith in the risen Christ. They need to be reminded that God has no grandchildren! The Bible only speaks of '*sons* of God'! Each generation has to find Christ for itself. A second-generation Christian is really a contradiction in terms. But the vast majority of members of the nominal churches have simply *drifted* into membership, or grown up into the faith without ever experiencing a time of decision or being born again. Hence they have no idea what it is to experience the presence and the power of Christ in their lives.

A major reason for the lack of spiritual power in many of the nominal churches is the lack of the central importance of the scriptures. In the work that I have been involved in for many years in the East End of London, we have re-opened a number of redundant churches closed by the major denominations as being of no further use to them. I well remember one big old Methodist church that we took over in the mid-1970s and which hadn't been used for worship for fifteen years. The great old church had a seating capacity of about eight hundred. It stood there in a semi-derelict state, a monument to the past, stained glass windows shattered, pews broken, furniture and fittings smashed by successive waves of vandals over the years of dereliction. The shrinking congregation had retreated into the hall, and had continued to grow smaller and smaller until they were down to the last handful and the church was finally closed by the circuit authorities.

Before we took responsibility for the premises, with the
intention of re-opening them as a centre for evangelism and
community involvement, I did a tour of inspection with
several members of my staff. After looking at the hall and
associated rooms we went into the church, clambering over
dirt-covered pews and mountains of rubbish, until finally we
picked our way to the door on the side of the pulpit normally
used by the minister. We found our way out into a heavily
cobwebbed corridor and entered what had at one time been
the minister's vestry. In the corner was a huge old iron safe.
One of us tried the handle and found it was locked. Out
of curiosity we began trying the keys from the large bunch
we had been given, to see whether one would fit. Eventually
the lock clicked over and the handle was turned. After much
heaving and straining the door noisily began to grind open.
We all stretched forward, craning our necks to see what
treasures were concealed in the huge old safe. As the door
was pulled open we all stood there dumb, in profound silence,
as we gazed upon the only thing in the safe – the great old
leather-bound pulpit Bible! We stood there for several
moments without speaking, deeply moved, for here was the
key to the closure of this church. The word of the Lord was
bound, locked up in that huge iron safe in a vestry behind
the pulpit. It seemed to us to be a parable symbolizing the
tragedy of the twentieth-century nominal church.

THE EVANGELICALS

One of the strange anomalies of the present situation of the
churches in Britain is that there are a great many evangelical
churches that are just as much stuck in a 'no growth rut'
as are the liberal churches that they so much despise. It would

be a gross over-simplification to suggest that growth is related to Biblical theology. It would be very nice and neat if we could show that all liberal churches were not growing and that all Bible-believing churches were. This would then give us a clear recipe for church growth. Such is not the case. In the United States current trends, indicated by church membership and attendance figures issued by all the denominations, suggest that attitudes to the scriptures *are* probably linked with growth. The figures suggest that it is the Bible-believing/evangelical churches that are growing, and the liberal churches that are not growing, or are even declining. In Britain this is not so.

It is certainly true that overall the liberal churches are declining, and declining rapidly, in all the protestant denominations. It is also true that the liberal theological colleges have been declining rapidly over the past twenty years, and that most of them have now closed. Of those that remain, some have only a handful of students, such as one liberal college that currently has only six students (rumour has it that four of them meet daily to pray for the conversion of the principal). On the other hand, the evangelical theological colleges and the Bible colleges are enjoying an unprecedented boom. Many of them are expanding rapidly, and the request for places far exceeds the number of students they can take.

We cannot, however, make a clear statement that most evangelical churches in Britain are growing. Some are, especially those in favoured suburbs such as those in the Home Counties or 'commuter belt' (sometimes known as the Bible belt) around Greater London. The real evidence of growth, however, is found amongst churches in the 'Renewal' or 'Charismatic' constituency. The use of these terms is, of course, open to misunderstanding, since there is no clear definition of 'renewal' or 'charismatic', and the terms are very loosely used in Britain today. They usually mean some form of belief in and exercise of the gifts of the Spirit, although the form of worship and church government may vary enormously. There are many churches in the liberal traditions of all the major denominations where the minister and members of the congregation have had a renewing spiritual experience in recent years, which has led them into the charismatic constituency at some point or other. What invariably happens is that their view of scripture changes radically. The Bible becomes vastly more important and is eagerly studied and searched. There is a strong desire to order worship and the life of the congregation upon a scriptural basis, and the word of God is given a new authority, both in the preaching and in the whole life of the corporate community of Christians in the local church.

Many churches that were formerly of a liberal tradition but that are now in the renewal constituency, have tended to associate themselves with churches in the evangelical or traditional Bible-believing constituency. In many cases they find that they have little in common except a love of the scriptures and their acceptance of the Bible as the authoritative word of God. Many churches in the renewal constituency have not signed and would not sign a doctrinal statement of belief. This is sometimes a stumbling block to fellowship with traditional evangelical churches, who like everyone to sign a clear, unequivocal statement of Biblical faith before entering into fellowship with them. It may, in fact, be this preoccupation with the finer points of Biblical doctrine, that undoubtedly arises out of the historical roots of protestantism in Britain, which provides a clue to the understanding of the no-growth situation in which many evangelical churches are stuck today.

Wherever there is an over-emphasis upon the defence of doctrine, the concern of the fellowship tends to centre upon the *letter* of the word rather than the *life* of the word. The result is that traditionalism gains the upper hand, and the fellowship tends to routinize all its practices, only allowing things to be done as they have always been done in the past. Clearly this is not only a recipe for unresponsiveness to the changing needs of a new generation of men and women. It is also an indication of unresponsiveness to any new revelation of truth through the ministry of the Holy Spirit and under the *authority of scripture*, by applying the unchanging word of God to the changing generations of mankind. There are three major areas where evangelicals in Britain today seem to be largely unresponsive to the needs and conditions of the closing decades of the twentieth century:

(1) The first is in the area of worship.
(2) The second is in the area of social conditions.
(3) The third is in the area of life style.

(1) Worship

Worship in many evangelical churches has become dull, lifeless and repetitious. The major concern appears to be to do things in exactly the same way as they were sixty or seventy years ago, in the heyday of evangelical revival. The assumption is that because it worked then it should work now. When it doesn't work and people don't come to join in worship or to hear the Gospel, preacher and congregation rationalize their failure by saying that people are unresponsive to the Gospel nowadays. The last thing they do is to question their presentation of the Gospel, or to ask themselves whether the diet of worship they are offering meets the needs of modern men, women and young people in the late twentieth century.

Many evangelical churches have lost the spirit of praise, overflowing joy and spontaneity in worship that characterizes the renewed churches of today, and which clearly was present in the halcyon days of revival. This was certainly true of the Wesleys, who sang their way through Britain, with songs of praise and an abundance of joy that lifted believers above the drab routine of everyday life into a living fellowship with the Lord. It was praise and a new dimension of worship that characterized the early Church, where members met together to share their joys in the Lord and to join together in the reality of the presence of the living Lord among them. Worship in the New Testament churches was not a dull routine in which minister and congregation played out their traditional roles, as in so many evangelical churches today; it was a joyous adventure of expectation, to which every believer contributed out of his own experience of the Lordship of Jesus in his own life. Worship that has lost that sense of expectation, wonder and awe through the realization of the presence of the Lord, becomes a dull, routine religious exercise. Many evangelicals need to learn again the meaning of praise. They could well learn from the charismatics what it is to be open to the Spirit so that their worship is characterized by reality rather than by routine, by enthusiasm and expectation rather than by a dour restatement of doctrine, and by life and growth rather than by faithful maintenance of tradition.

(2) *Social Conditions*

Many evangelicals have shown almost a callous lack of concern for social conditions in Britain in recent years. It is worth recording that this was not always so, and that historically the Labour movement itself grew out of the deep social concern and prophetic ministries of some of the great Bible-believing Non-Conformist preachers of the nineteenth century. The great divide between evangelicals and social action Christians is a blasphemy of the modern Church, and certainly does not even go back as far as the previous century, let alone have any foundation in Biblical tradition.

There are three basic elements in Biblical tradition that

evangelicals need to grapple with if they are to be effective in bringing the Gospel to bear upon the great social issues of our day. They are:

(a) a concern for social justice
(b) a concern for equality
(c) a concern for the individual

(a) A CONCERN FOR SOCIAL JUSTICE

The Christian faith is firmly founded upon a concept of a just society. From Genesis to Revelation God is revealed in the scriptures as a God of justice and righteousness. God condemned without reservation the murder of Abel by his brother Cain. From Joshua to Samuel the judges laboured to establish justice amongst the Israelites in the land of Canaan. Through the great eighth-century prophets the word of the Lord thundered against the oppressors of the poor, who sold the children of their debtors into slavery, and against the corrupt judges who took bribes from the rich and gave no justice to the poor. Jesus warned those who exploited the widows and the underprivileged, while James exhorted the Christians in the early Church that their duty was not simply to *preach* the Gospel but to *do* something about the conditions of the poor and the deprived.

If we are to proclaim and to live a full Gospel there has to be a real concern for social justice at the heart of the life of the Christian Church. There has to be a determination to proclaim the word of the Lord to an unjust society, to join in the struggles of the poor and the powerless, to proclaim judgement against the oppressors, whether they be the wealthy landowners or the big labour union bosses. There has to be a willingness to accept suffering in the name of the Lord in the cause of justice. It is this *prophetic role* that the Church has abdicated for far too long.

The Gospel is not the means of legitimizing the life styles

and positions of social privilege of the rich and the powerful!
Yet in some wealthy evangelical churches this is precisely
what it has become.

Jesus drew his followers from the humble poor who 'heard
him gladly'. Today in Britain, amongst the ordinary working
people, his Church is viewed as part of 'the Establishment'
– the power structure of the nation. Ministers have usually
come from the privileged classes, or at least when they have
come from working-class families they have been trained to
take their place amongst the educated elite of society. This
is what is expected of them, so it is little wonder that few
of them are willing to renounce the comfortable way of life
and live amongst the poor in the inner city, sharing the lot
of the powerless and the deprived, and championing their
cause in the name of the God of justice. In fact it often
causes some bewilderment when Christians do champion the
cause of the poor.

On one occasion during my ministry in the East End, I
appeared for the defence in the appeal court on behalf of
a young black who had been convicted of being involved
in a robbery. He was a boy with a bad record but who came
from a beautiful Christian family, and he was trying
desperately hard to change his life. I was convinced that he
was innocent on this particular occasion, and there was
strong evidence that the police were out to get him and that
their evidence was false. He had been arrested three times
in one week without any charges being preferred against him.
The appeal was, in fact, upheld and the conviction against
him quashed. But the thing that astonished me was that the
lawyer for the police tried to discredit my evidence by
alleging that I was some kind of extremist political revolutionary. He suggested that he had evidence that I was a
member of a Marxist group in east London. I was able to
declare that I was not and never had been a member of any
political party. In fact, this accusation gave me the oppor-

tunity to witness to my faith. I stated in no uncertain terms that, far from being a political activist, I was a Christian minister involved in mission in the inner city precisely because I did not believe that salvation would come through political programmes but only through Jesus Christ.

The very fact that this attack was levelled at me I saw as significant. It is surely an indictment upon the Christian Church that when a minister stands up for the poor and the oppressed he is accused of being a political revolutionary! Are Marxists the only ones who care for the poor? What has happened to Christian witness in our land? What has happened to our Biblical tradition? What has happened to our prophetic task? 'Let justice roll down like waters and righteousness like an ever-flowing stream' (Amos 5:24; R.S.V.).

(b) A CONCERN FOR EQUALITY

The Christian concept of a just society is founded upon the belief that all men are equal before God. Paul's basic dictum for unity and equality in the early Church was, 'There is neither Jew nor Greek, there is neither slave nor free, there is neither male nor female; for you are all one in Christ Jesus' (Galatians 3:28). For Paul the social distinctions of a sinful society were irrelevant. There were only two classes, the saved and the unsaved – those who knew the Lord and those who did not, those who were members of the household of faith and those who were outside it. For those who were 'in Christ' the social distinctions of race, sex, status, family and social class were utterly meaningless and were barriers to fellowship in the fullness of Christ. Thus he commands Philemon to receive back Onesimus, the runaway slave, who had been converted not 'as a slave but . . . as a beloved brother' (Philemon 16).

This equality experienced by those who are 'in Christ' stems from their relationship to the Lord They know them selves to be equally loved by God as sinners for whom Christ died. But for the Christian it is not enough simply to love other Christians. Christ's commandment is to love *all* men. The Christian, therefore, sees all men as equally loved by God and seeks to bring them all into that relationship with God known as being 'in Christ'. The Christian does not wait until men are converted until he accords them equality. He remembers that 'while we were yet sinners Christ died for us', the ungodly (Romans 5:6, 8). There are three elements of equality desperately needed in Britain today that derive from a Biblical understanding of society.

(i) The first is equality of **status**. In God's wisdom he has made a different distribution of gifts to all mankind. These gifts should determine our *function* but NOT our *status* in life. The two are linked in a secular society but not in a Christian one. In the fellowship of the Church the bank manager sits down with the road sweeper and the two are one in Christ. In the fellowship of believers there are no *social* distinctions, only distinctions of *spiritual* gifts.

(ii) The second is equality of **rights and obligations**. Everyone in the ideal Christian society has an equality of rights and obligations. This is similar to the rights and obligations we share within the Christian family. In our home where there is love for one another, these rights and obligations are mutually recognized. If we carry the analogy over into society it means that *all* should share in the decision-making processes of society – each according to his ability. All should have a right to the exercise of power, as well as an obligation to use their gifts for the good of all.

(iii) The third is equality of **opportunity**. The Christian society should be structured in a way that enables each individual to have access to life chances commensurate with his abilities. A just society accords equality of opportunity to all, irrespective of race, sex and social position. The Christian Church, as the bearer of the Gospel, has to work for (and to be *seen* to be working for) a just society built upon the foundations of equality. This is not an optional extra of the Gospel, it is a *commandment* of God for, 'He has showed you, O man, what is good; and what does the Lord require of you but to do justice, and to love kindness, and to walk humbly with your God?' (Micah 6:8).

(c) A CONCERN FOR THE INDIVIDUAL

At the heart of the Gospel there is a deep concern for the worth of each individual. John says, 'God so loved the *world*, that he gave his only begotten son' (John 3:16). But it was not just a love for the world as a mass of people. John goes on, '*Whosoever* believes in him should not perish, but have everlasting life.' Salvation is not a mass social process, it is offered to each one as an individual. This amazing love of God for each of his children is beyond our human under-standing. Jesus tells us that he knows us so well that he even knows the number of the hairs on our head. He knows every detail of our lives and he cares for us beyond our under-standing.

One of the most devastating effects of our modern social order is the way it 'de-personalizes' the individual. A major characteristic of our modern Western civilization is that complex social forces combine to reduce people to a sense of powerlessness and personal insignificance – especially in the great urban and industrial centres of life. For some people everything in life seems to rob them of any real sense of significance. If you are poor, or a member of an ethnic minority, if you have low education, or are living on welfare, or struggling to bring up a family without a husband, or living on the twenty-third floor of a concrete tower block, or doing a dull, boring, repetitive job in a factory production line, it's difficult to discern real meaning and purpose in life.

Millions of people in the inner city lack a sense of personal identity. They feel that somehow they don't belong. They are just a number on a card index in a giant filing system in a vast, bureaucratically controlled, impersonal society. They suffer from what the sociologist knows as 'anomie'. It is a malaise of the 'non-belongingness' peculiar to the modern inner city, that no politician, social philosopher or reformer has been able successfully to combat.

The Gospel is *good news* for the alienated urban multitudes. The Gospel does not recognize masses, it sees only individuals beloved by God, people for whom Christ died. The gospel record of Jesus dealing with individuals is the core of our faith. Whether he was dealing with a blind beggar, an outcast leper or a madman, whether he was going to the bedside of a sick child or to comfort a friend whose brother had died, or whether he was himself dying on the cross, he showed the same loving concern for people as individuals. Even when the crowds were pressing around him he was sensitive to the needs of one woman who touched him. Jesus looked beyond the rough exterior to the inner man. He saw the *potential* in each individual. He saw the Peter in Simon, the Matthew in Levi, the Mary Magdalene in the woman taken in adultery, the Paul in Saul of Tarsus. But Jesus not only saw the potential in people, he also had the power to change lives, to bring that potential into reality. The transforming power of the living Christ meant *new life* for every believer.

This is the way Jesus transforms the life of whole communities – through the lives of changed people. When you are 'in Christ' you are a part of the new community – his new creation. In the new community we belong to each other because we belong to God. It is through our relationship to God as Father that we are brought into a relationship of brother and sister with our fellow men and women, of every race and social position. We are brought into this relationship with the Father through Jesus Christ.

It is through witness to this basic truth of the Gospel that evangelicals have a contribution of immense significance to make to the evangelization of Britain today. If the main thrust of any new evangelistic outreach into society is simply a redoubling of effort in social caring, it will founder in disaster. Of course Christians must care. But caring is an *outcome* of the Gospel, not the Gospel itself! The Gospel is the good news that through Jesus Christ we can enter into a living relationship with God our Creator, and thereby enter into new life. The Gospel promises the forgiveness of sins for the individual and a new basis of life through Christ, a new joy, a new inner peace and a new power through the Holy Spirit. Evangelicals have a historic witness to the great central truths of the Gospel that are desperately needed in Britain today. It is the only power of salvation. This is not simply 'an evangelical Gospel'. It is THE Gospel – there is no other! A so-called 'social Gospel' is not a Gospel at all. At best it is a mere humanitarian creed that has no power to transform society. Societies are not transformed by creeds and philosophies, or by programmes of reform, however well intentioned and however soundly morally based. Societies are made up of individuals, and it is when the lives of individuals are changed radically and fundamentally by a spiritual power that overcomes their predisposition towards evil that they receive the power and impetus to change society.

If the Church ever stops proclaiming both the need for individual rebirth and that salvation is only in the Name of Jesus, it will have ceased to preach the Gospel of the New Testament. But we must beware of separating the Gospel into 'spiritual' and 'social' elements. Jesus did not. He proclaimed a whole Gospel that was not simply contained in words but that issued in a way of life. Evangelicals have to beware of the danger of being so concerned with *proclaiming* the Gospel that they cease to *live* it! These are the words of our Lord in Matthew 25:

> Then the King will say to those at his right hand, 'Come, O blessed of my Father, inherit the kingdom prepared for you from the foundation of the world; for I was hungry and you gave me food, I was thirsty and you gave me drink, I was a stranger and you welcomed me, I was naked and you clothed me, I was sick and you visited me, I was in prison and you came to me.' Then the righteous will answer him, 'Lord, when did we see thee hungry and feed thee, or thirsty and give thee drink? And when did we see thee a stranger and welcome thee, or naked and clothe thee? And when did we see thee sick or in prison and visit thee?' And the King will answer them, 'Truly, I say to you, as you did it to one of the least of my brethren, you did it to me' (Matthew 25:34–40).

(3) *Life Style*

Communication is a perennial problem for human beings. How can we be sure that the words we speak convey the message we are trying to communicate? There is nothing more frustrating than knowing your words have been misunderstood, that you have not been heard. The temptation is simply to shout louder or to protest. The only effect this has, apart from relieving our own feelings, is to widen the communication gap, not bridge it. Under these circumstances what we need to do is to review the whole method of communication. It may be that we are not using the wrong words to communicate the message but that there are other impedimenta, some other barriers that are blocking the communication process. It may be that what we *are* is speaking louder than what we *say*. Perhaps people are trying to say to us, 'I can't hear what you say because of what you *are*!'

This is sometimes the situation between evangelical Christians and others.

The life style of evangelical Christians can sometimes act as a barrier to communication with others. The Biblical concept of holiness, which is so important to evangelicals, inevitably results in a measure of separation. But holiness in its Biblical roots means *separation to* rather than *separation from*. The vessels used in the Temple are a good example of the Biblical understanding of holiness. They were 'holy unto the Lord' – set apart from ordinary everyday, common usage, separated unto the Lord, used exclusively in his service. In the prophetic tradition the nation Israel was also holy in this same sense, separated unto the Lord, consecrated into his service. But in the true prophetic tradition Israel was to be 'a light unto the nations', her separation was not *from* the world but *to the Lord*. She was chosen by God and consecrated for service among the nations. Her task would be fulfilled when in the day of the Lord all the nations would come to a knowledge of him and to the true worship of God. 'It shall come to pass in the latter days that the mountain of the house of the Lord shall be established as the highest of the mountains, and shall be raised above the hills; and all the nations shall flow to it' (Isaiah 2:2 and Micah 4:1).

Holiness can so easily be mistaken for exclusiveness and as the establishment of a form of elitism that is a separation *from* others, acting as a barrier to the communication of the Gospel. Where our life style becomes elitist it is not holy, indeed it is quite the reverse, for the Lord is not able to use us in his service if we are separated from our non-Christian neighbours. If we allow our life style to develop into a form of moral exclusiveness it acts primarily as a barrier to communication with non-Christians. When this happens, the Church becomes an 'in-group', where the members are able to satisfy their spiritual and social needs through the life of

the fellowship, but have less and less to do with people outside
it. There is the classic case of the church that was considering
growth, and one of the means decided upon was to hold a
supper party to which the members would invite their non-
Christian friends. The whole scheme failed because one after
another the members confessed that they had no non-
Christian friends!

The church that develops into a cosy, exclusive spiritual
club is certainly not able to respond to Jesus' great commandment, 'Go into all the world and make disciples' (see
Matthew 28:19). We need to be vitally in touch with the
world around us if we are to save it. God's purpose is to use
us as channels through which he can communicate his truth,
his love and his saving power to the world, but so often we
are like wood and stone are to electricity – very poor con-
ductors.

There is cost involved in this mission. Mission is the meeting point of the incarnation and the cross. 'God so loved the
world that he gave ...' (John 3:16). 'He emptied himself,
taking the form of a servant, being born in the likeness of
men. And being found in human form he humbled himself
and became obedient unto death, even death on a cross'
(Philippians 2:7–8). Mission involves identifying ourselves
with the sinful world around us, of which we are a part. But
it is an identification for service. We are called to be 'in' but
not 'of' a sinful society. Mission *is* a costly business. It involves
sacrifice – the sacrifice of one's own self-interest. Identification with a sinful society means actually experiencing the
burden of guilt and opening it up to the forgiving, redeeming
power of Christ. This involves us in suffering, just as it did
Jesus.

All too often evangelical Christians have not been prepared
to pay the price of mission in our modern world. Certainly
in the inner-city areas of Britain they have been conspicuous
by their absence. They have fled the city and left it to the

devil to take the hindmost. One after another, inner-city churches have closed throughout all the conurbations, or it has been left to the liberal Christians, with their predominantly social action witness, to continue any form of Christian presence. Evangelicals have not identified with the struggles of the poor and the oppressed in the name of Christ. They have not stood alongside their black brothers and sisters and said, 'In the name of Jesus we are with you. Your fight is our fight. We love you because Jesus died for you. He broke down the barriers between the races and made us one, therefore we will struggle with you for equality and for a just society.' Evangelicals have largely forgotten that Jesus was born in a stable, into a poor peasant carpenter's family, and that it was from the lowly status of unfashionable Nazareth that he came to proclaim the Gospel, saying, 'The time is fulfilled, and the kingdom of God is at hand; repent, and believe in the gospel' (Mark 1:15).

Evangelicals need to remember that we have to earn the right to a hearing of the Gospel in our modern world. When we remain in our places of privilege we are placing a barrier between ourselves and our brothers and sisters in the Third World, or in the great inner-city populations of our urban industrial societies in the West, for all of whom Christ died. Incarnational Christianity means putting ourselves at risk. It means sacrificing our privileged life styles and identifying with the deprived and the powerless, in order to become channels of the creative power of Christ, who alone can change men and through their changed lives re-create society into the pattern of the kingdom. All too often evangelicals have thought of the communication of the Gospel as a simple matter of proclamation in words. They have not fully understood the theology of the incarnation, and the obligation upon the followers of Jesus to become his body here in the city where the struggle is intense or there in the 'out-back' where there is ignorance and fear. God has so ordained the ordering of his creation that Christ has no hands but our hands to do his work on earth.

Summary

The evidence we have been examining has shown something of the movement of spiritual renewal that is gaining strength and momentum in Britain. At the same time we have had to recognize that there are powerful forces of destruction at work in our society. We saw something of these in previous chapters, but in this chapter noted that the destructive forces were, in fact, creating a new opportunity for the proclamation of the Gospel in Britain. The third way is the work of the Holy Spirit in our nation, bringing 'times of refreshment' to a spiritually dry and barren land. Whether or not there will be a great spiritual revival in our land is to some extent linked with the readiness of the people of God to respond to the promptings of his Spirit. Are the Christians in Britain open to the Holy Spirit and eager to seize the opportunity to be used by God, in what could well be one of the most fundamentally creative (or *re*-creative!) periods in the history of mankind?

In attempting to answer this question we looked at the situation in our churches of both the liberal and the evangelical traditions. Basically we saw that Christians of the liberal theological traditions have a strong sense of social justice, which they derive from the Gospel, and a desire to witness through their lives in the world, but that they lack the authority of the Lordship of Jesus over their lives and witness. This authority derives from a personal encounter with Christ and a continuing experience of living under the reality of the presence of the risen Lord. Liberal Christians are usually deeply concerned with 'kingdom building', but they often tend to regard this in terms of programmes of action carried out in our own human strength, rather than as radical spiritual movements of re-creation directed by the power of the Holy Spirit. Individual salvation, which is the essence of the Gospel, tends to play a less important part in the thinking of liberal Christians than does their social action programme.

The evangelical Christians, on the other hand, have the Gospel centrally in their thinking but are often unconcerned with, or ineffective in, social witness. The application of the Gospel to the social conditions of man, or to the structures of society, is often considered irrelevant and many evangelicals believe that their prime task is the *proclamation*, rather than the living out, of the practical implications of the Gospel. There is a tendency for evangelical Christians to become insulated from social issues and to concern themselves solely with verbal witness. In practice this reduces the effectiveness of communication in the modern world, and often results in a lack of outreach, so that some churches are simply a diminishing number of Christians telling each other the Gospel.

Tradition can become a binding force, and some churches in both the liberal and evangelical traditions are stuck in no-growth situations bound by the shackles of tradition. They are unable to respond to changing circumstances because they are firmly anchored in the past. Tradition is the final authority and they are therefore not open to the direction of the Holy Spirit or expecting God to do anything new. They are something like the church at Ephesus when Paul arrived there, which had not heard of the Holy Spirit. These churches have *heard* of the Holy Spirit but they don't *know* him. They have read of him and they sing about him, but they have never actually experienced him!

Churches in the 'renewal' or 'charismatic' constituency have experienced the presence, the power and the gifts of the Holy Spirit, but many have cast away tradition to such an extent that they lack the authority and stability that derive from a scripturally based tradition, they have become purely experiential, and if experience does not accord with scripture then it is scripture that is ignored.

Perhaps if Christians in each of the traditions, Evangelical, Liberal and Renewal, were to give to each other their essential spiritual insights – the Evangelical their emphasis upon individual salvation through Christ, the Liberal their deep concern for the application of the Gospel ethic to the great social issues of our day, and the Charismatic their vital experience of the power of the Holy Spirit – perhaps then we could have a full Gospel making its impact upon the life of our nation. Maybe what is needed today is a Biblically-based renewal movement with a prophetic concern for people, for justice, truth and righteousness; for translating the Gospel into a living reality in the structures of society.

Maybe such a Biblically-based renewal movement would give us a new approach to evangelism that would carry the Gospel through our land with the dynamic power of the Holy Spirit as its driving force. It would enable us to get away from the old-style traditional proclamation of the Gospel of individual salvation, that has been the hallmark of evangelical revivalism throughout this century. With the new emphasis upon praise and adoration in worship, the Holy Spirit is opening up to us a new dimension in evangelism in presenting the Gospel message within an act of praise and the celebration of the Lordship of Jesus. Perhaps during the closing years of this century we shall increasingly see 'Festivals of Praise' replace the evangelistic mission, or 'Celebration Evangelism' replace crusade evangelism. It may well be that the Lord is teaching us a spiritual lesson we need to learn: that the most effective form of evangelism is when we allow the Holy Spirit himself to speak to the hearts of non-believers. *He* does the evangelism instead of us. We simply praise God and give him all the glory, and his power, the power of the Holy Spirit, is poured out. Jesus said, 'I, if I be lifted up . .

will draw all men unto me' (John 12:32; A.V.). There is an attractive power in the Name of Jesus. When we glorify him he draws men to him as Saviour and they accept him as Lord.

But how much time have we? How much time do we have before our civilization goes spinning out of control, driven by the forces of destruction that are propelling it? Maybe it's too late for any form of evangelism. It may be that the forces of moral, spiritual and social decay are too advanced to be halted by anything other than the direct intervention of God. Unless the people of God are aware of the realities of the situation, are open to the Holy Spirit, prepared to be obedient to the Lord and to take up a prophetic task in the nation, the forces of darkness and destruction may well overwhelm us.

In the final chapter we shall examine these great issues in the light of the evidence so far amassed.

THE
FORCES OF LIGHT
AND DARKNESS

Where there is no prophecy the people cast
off restraint.

Proverbs 29:18
(Revised Standard Version)

CHAPTER SIX

THE FORCES OF LIGHT
AND DARKNESS

Harvey Cox in *The Secular City*[23] believes that we are at the end of the religious era of mankind, speaking of the 'passing of Christendom and the emergence of a highly differentiated secular civilization'. There is much to support this analysis, and volumes could be written tracing the sources of secularization. Equally it could be amply demonstrated that resultantly we live in an age of unsurpassed tension and conflict, both for the individual and the wider society. Every aspect of the media, from the daily news to the world of modern art, expresses something of the violence and confusion of the age in which we live.

Nevertheless, Harvey Cox may not be right in forecasting the end of Christendom. This certainly does not accord with a Biblical world view, which anticipates a time when the forces of light and the forces of darkness will clash head on. Jesus spoke of nation rising against nation, and of a time of great turmoil and suffering which would herald the end of the age and the time when God would establish the kingdom.

There can be no denying that we are in the midst of an age of conflict. The history of the twentieth century so far has been written in blood. Of course, every century has had its wars. The twentieth century does not mark the beginning of violence. Indeed, the whole history of mankind could be described as the record of human conflict. But what is unique about the present century is the massive advances in technology and the application of it to the business of destruction. Hence we have seen global wars, mass destruction, mass slaughter, indiscriminate cruelty, senseless violence. We have produced weapons capable of destroying all living matter and annihilating the human race. As the century moves towards its close so we are being driven inexorably towards the point of ultimate crisis. But what does this mean for the future of mankind? How are we to interpret the signs of the times?

Summary of Analysis

In our analysis of the social processes at work in modern Britain we have established that the forces of social change are rapidly moving towards the point of social disintegration. The political and economic forces are also moving towards a point of crisis. The total effect of what is being produced is a highly dynamic and volatile social situation which will either erupt in political revolution or result in the degeneration of society to the point of disintegration of organized social life.

We have also noted a third force at work in Britain today, and that is the power of spiritual renewal which is beginning to move through our country. It is this power that is bringing new life and new hope to thousands of new Christians, who have turned to Jesus as providing the only answer to both the individual and the corporate problems of society.

Our analysis has shown that there are three broad streams of action or 'forces' at work in our nation. They are like three powerful high speed trains, all moving rapidly in the same direction along parallel tracks. But the tracks are not completely parallel, there is a point of convergence where they meet and cross over. The question is, which one will reach the intersection first, will two reach it at the same moment, or will all three get there together? The race is on!

What will be the result?

If we transfer that analogy to our three forces the question becomes, 'Will there be political revolution, social breakdown or spiritual revival?' Another alternative is that social breakdown and political revolution may occur at the same time. Or it may be that all three forces are on a collision course and may occur simultaneously. That would be a truly apocalyptic event, a clash of the forces of good and evil, the battle of light and darkness for the mastery of mankind.

In order to come to a right assessment of the situation so that we may prophesy the future (or, for sociologists, 'predict the likely outcome') let us just briefly recapitulate the salient points of our analysis.

We have looked at the activism of political extremists of both the Right and the Left. We have noted the continuing pressures on the economy of chronic inflation and of the increasing tensions between management and workers throughout industry. We have noted the growing violence on our streets and a steadily increasing threat to the maintenance of law and order in the inter-racial and inter-ethnic conflicts that occur in our cities. We have seen the failure of our education system to provide the basic essentials for social mobility in an increasingly affluent society. This results in a denial of access to social and economic goals for millions of young people growing up in the inner city, who feel trapped within a social class setting that has many characteristics of a caste situation. Add to this the fact of race or colour or other physically distinguishing characteristics, and the result is a potentially dangerous situation that can at any moment erupt into the kind of violence that has been seen on many city streets throughout the world in recent years.

When people feel trapped in a social situation that denies them access to what they believe are basic fundamental rights, and where the mass media and glossy magazines continually flaunt the apparent affluence and power of others, the frustration developed among the disprivileged, who are relatively deprived, eventually grows to uncontainable proportions. The drama that is being played out in the inner-city areas of the great conurbations throughout Britain is the vanguard of the gathering storm. It is not yet clear whether what we are already witnessing are the opening salvoes of political revolution, or the early warning phenomenology of social disintegration. But what is abundantly clear is that there are many people who are only too ready to make use of the social and economic plight of the nation to help create the kind of situation in which a political revolution could succeed.

In terms of social processes we have noted that we are living in days of exceptionally rapid change, when all our traditions and customs, as well as our beliefs and values, are being challenged in an unprecedented manner. This inevitably has its effect upon the stability of society. The forces of social change, blowing like whirlwinds through our society, create not only social tensions but also a high level of personal insecurity for millions of people. This is evidenced by the fact that more than half of all the beds in the Health Service institutions throughout the country are occupied by patients suffering from psychiatric disorders. In an age when everything in life is changing rapidly, from the old familiar physical environment of streets and shops and buildings, through to the stability of the family as the core institution in our society, it is inevitable that the effect upon the mental health and stability of the nation must be one of enormous strain.

People need security, the security of belonging and the security of belief. The security of belonging to a nation, to a community and to a family gives identity to each individual and a basic structure to society. The security of belief in an ordered universe, in the ultimacy of fundamental values such as righteousness, justice, truth and love, together with the belief that there is meaning and purpose underlying the whole of life, both here and beyond the grave, give to both the individual and to society as such an orderliness and a stable framework for the whole of life.

Fundamental Values

Security of belonging and of belief provides the foundation of being both for man as an individual and for man in community. But such foundations are not *sui generis* – they derive from 'the ultimate ground of all being' (to use Paul Tillich's phrase), that is, from God himself and not from within man. We are not simply arguing that man needs God. This would be to fall into Durkheimian pragmatism. (Durkheim argued that each society produces the form of religion that suits its own social needs.) We are simply stating the belief that ultimate values derive from God, the source of all created life and matter.

It is the value system which lies at the foundations of the structure of society that has been fundamentally affected and shaken by the forces of change at work in Britain today. Our analysis has revealed that modern man is lost in a world of his own creating, a world in which he has let loose forces which he is powerless to control, forces that threaten to destroy his individual sanity and his social existence. Under such circumstances only the intervention of a power greater than man himself, a power that is in control of the fundamental forces of creation, can transform the situation.

This is not, however, to give the impression that all social change is bad. There have been a great many significant social changes in Britain this century that have brought immense benefit to ordinary men and women. Major improvements in the physical conditions of life for millions of people have resulted from basic changes in the structure and organization of society. If the social structure is unjust, and because of it many are deprived of basic rights while others exploit and enjoy unbridled luxury, then the social system needs to be changed. If the social system is based upon a culture that is immoral and exposes children to various forms of moral danger, then there need to be some radical changes in that society.

In the same way, we would not want to give the impression that all radical political change should be opposed by Christians. Indeed the reverse is the truth. If the Gospel were to be put into practice in any modern Western society it would bring about radical political changes. Jesus had compassion on the poor and the powerless. He identified with them and they heard his good news gladly. Jesus warned the exploiters, the rich and the powerful, that they were in danger of God's judgement upon them. But Jesus did not advocate the way of violent revolution as the way of overthrowing a corrupt political regime. His was the way of love, of the cross, of redemptive suffering. 'Blessed are the meek for they shall inherit the earth ... Blessed are the peacemakers for they shall be called the children of God.' It was not that Jesus saw no need for revolutionary change. It was the *method* of the revolution that he revolutionized. 'For whoever would save his life will lose it; and whoever loses his life for my sake and the gospel's will save it' (Mark 8:35; R.S.V.).

The crux of the problem confronting Britain today is not that there are no revolutionary changes needed, but that we lack a yardstick to measure what is good and what is bad. Without such a yardstick, or fixed point of reference, or absolute moral and spiritual standard, we have no means of gauging what changes are harmful to society and what is needed for our good. It is the fundamental conviction of the writer that such a yardstick is to be found, and only to be found, in the word of God as revealed in scripture. Despite all the problems of translation, textual criticism and inter- pretation, the Bible presents us with the authentic word of God. The God who is revealed in scripture as the God of creation has the only answer to our needs today, when we stand on the brink of destroying the creation of his hands, the environment and social order that have evolved around man, with the additional possibility of the total annihilation of all living matter including mankind itself. Such is the destructive power of the forces that are now gaining momen- tum in the world.

In summary, man's situation is desperate. His civilization is crumbling from its foundations. All too few people are aware of the acuteness of the danger. We are like the citizens of Sodom and Gomorrah, who went about their normal every- day business and social intercourse sublimely oblivious of the destructive forces about to engulf them and which would swallow up the entire cities and their citizens. The forces about to overwhelm and destroy us are not the physical forces of earthquake and fire, or wind and water, but the less tangible yet equally pernicious forces of social, economic, moral and spiritual decay. These are the forces that Paul has in mind when he sees that the real nature of the conflict facing man- kind is not a fight against flesh and blood but against the forces of spiritual evil at work within the universe. Thus the conflict in which we are involved is not simply a battle for improving social conditions and establishing social justice. Neither is it a fight for the survival of Western civilization or for the mere preservation of physical life from ultimate destruction. It is the ancient battle of good and evil, of right and wrong, of light and darkness, the forces of God and the forces of the Evil One.

What of the Future?

There are two outstanding dangers facing us as a nation:
the forces of destruction and the weakness of the Church.

(1) The Forces of Destruction

The forces that are threatening to destroy us as a nation are
well advanced. The socio-economic forces that have been
gathering momentum over the past quarter of a century have
now reached a stage in which, humanly speaking, it is impossible to arrest them. They have been allowed to reach this
stage not through deliberate economic, political or social
decisions, but through the build-up effects of human avarice
and sinfulness. We are in a situation such as Paul describes
with penetrating insight in Ephesians 6, where he sees that
the real battle is not against human agencies but 'against
the world rulers of this present darkness, against the spiritual
hosts of wickedness in the heavenly places'. In other words
the real conflict is basically spiritual rather than economic,
social, political or even moral. It is a spiritual battle in
which our world is being driven by powers of evil that are
outside our human control but which we aid and abet
through our sinfulness. We cannot resist them with our
human strength but only with the spiritual strength that God
supplies.

Britain is a sick society. Never has there been so much
evidence of dishonesty, corruption and evil practice in the life
of the nation. That is not to say that there was ever a day
when Britain was in a state of pristine purity, and then
suddenly in the present generation we have fallen from grace.
It is impossible to say whether there is more actual dishonesty
in the nation today than there was one hundred years ago or
two hundred years ago. In any case, such comparisons are

of little use. But what we can assert is that there is more *evidence* of corruption. The mass media see to this!

Day after day we are bombarded with the evidence of evil in our society. The media give massive coverage to all kinds of immorality, sexual deviance, homosexuality, abortion, disregard for the sanctity of life, violence, greed, cruelty, prejudice, discrimination, injustice, oppression, bribery and corruption. There is in the life of the nation an inevitable consequence of the constant exposure of the population to such matters. Gradually they become less and less shocking, they become more and more accepted as the norm, the general standard of behaviour. We become adjusted to them and in time we begin to adjust our own behaviour accordingly, concluding that as they represent the normal standards of behaviour of the nation we ourselves ought to conform. Thus over a period the behaviour of the nation and its basic social values and ethics undergo a radical change. In time even the voice of protest from those who hold traditional Christian values becomes dulled and muted. We feel powerless to resist the onslaught of secular forces, and gradually give way to the weight of supposedly popular opinion.

A new phenomenon of modern history is the role of the mass media in communicating new values and effecting radical social change through changing social values. It is an entirely new social phenomenon to see the culture of a nation change in a single generation as radically as ours has in Britain. Yet we must not give the impression that we ascribe this basic cultural change primarily to the action of impersonal evolutionary forces of social change.

In philosophical terms there is something deliberately purposive about the forces of social change working through our society. When a spirit of evil grips a community or nation there is a collective spiritual force of evil that drives it. That is precisely what has been happening in our nation in an age when the forces of secularization and technological

advance have coalesced to produce a situation in which man
has deliberately turned away from belief in a personal
Creator God and to a secular humanist world view. The
consequences of this choice are plain to see in the forces of
violence and social decay that have been set in motion.
Britain is in the vanguard of the Western world's drift towards
destruction.

Ours is a nation that has *chosen* to disregard God. We have
had the Gospel for centuries. The whole of our heritage is
rich with Christian tradition and with the things that bring
to man's awareness the presence of God. Yet we live in a
Godless age, in a generation that denies the very existence
of God and in which men have chosen to go their own way
and to ignore the commandments of God. They have chosen
to disregard the way of righteousness and to walk in the
ways of unrighteousness, and as a consequence they are
driven by the powers of evil that we have seen to be operating as an invisible force in the life of our nation.

When a nation becomes so evil that it deliberately chooses
to flout the laws of God and to adulate every kind of
corruption, there comes a point where God simply gives
them over to their wicked ways. He allows them to be driven
by the forces of destruction that will eventually sweep them
away. This is the most devastating judgement that God can
pronounce. He has abandoned the evil-doers and left them to
their own devices, knowing what their end will be. Paul
writes about this in Romans chapter 1, where he says that
'the wrath of God is revealed from heaven against all un-
godliness and wickedness of men who by their wickedness
suppress the truth. For what can be known about God is
plain to them, because God has shown it to them.' Despite
God having revealed himself to men they have deliberately
spurned him and chosen to live godless and wicked lives.
'Therefore God *gave them up* in the lusts of their hearts to
impurity, to the dishonouring of their bodies among them-

selves, because they exchanged the truth about God for a lie and worshipped and served the creature rather than the Creator, who is blessed for ever! Amen. For this reason God gave them up to dishonourable passions. Their women exchanged natural relations for unnatural, and the men likewise gave up natural relations with women and were consumed with passion for one another, men committing shameless acts with men and receiving in their own persons the due penalty for their error' (Romans 1:18–19, 24–27).

The strange anomaly is that the vast majority of people in Britain today claim to believe in God. They have a vague awareness of a Supreme Being but their whole manner of living is a denial of God. They do not acknowledge his authority. As far as they are concerned he is completely irrelevant. They act as though he cannot see them and as though it doesn't matter what they do. Whilst claiming to believe in him, they act as though he was not their Creator. The words of Isaiah speak to such a situation: 'Woe to those who hide deep from the Lord their counsel, whose deeds are in the dark, and who say, "Who sees us? Who knows us?" You turn things upside down! Shall the potter be regarded as the clay; that the thing made should say of its maker, "He did not make me"; or the thing formed say of him who formed it, "He has no understanding"?' (Isaiah 29:15–16).

Because God is a God of justice he cannot tolerate the deliberate rebelliousness of mankind. Our nation has drifted further and further from the truth and strayed away from the paths of righteousness that are clearly set out in the word of God. Hence the wrath of God is stirred against men. The wrath of God is not a blind irrational rage. It is a righteous indignation at the deliberate waywardness and disobedience of his children. Jesus himself speaks about the wrath of God. He says, 'He who believes in the Son has eternal life; he who does not obey the Son shall not see life, but the wrath of God rests upon him' (John 3:36). That word 'rests' indicates a continuous action, the wrath of God *stays* on man. It will not be withdrawn unless there is real repentance and a total change in the whole way of life of the nation.

It is the *nation* that has now come under the wrath of God and that is why we are experiencing such terrible times. That is why there is such turmoil in the life of the country. That is why there is conflict, violence and lawlessness, crime and vice, insecurity and unrest. We imagine that our problems are economic and social but at root they are *spiritual*. We shall never control inflation until man's selfishness and greed have been conquered, and this is a spiritual problem. At root it has its origins in the values of our society, and these values stem from the realm of ultimate reality. We imagine that our social problems are related to the issues of law and order, but at root they are spiritual problems deriving from man's sinful nature, his wilful disregard of his neighbour and of God's law that we should love one another. But it is just no use telling people that they must love one another, be nice and kind to one another, so long as they are driven by the forces of evil. They will simply laugh and jeer, and tell you that being kind and unselfish gets you nowhere. 'You have to look after yourself in this life because nobody else will.' They will tell you that everybody else is being dishonest and cheating one another, so why shouldn't they? – they have to look after their own interests.

Man is being driven by the forces of evil that are outside his control, and our nation is well advanced on the road to destruction. We are under the wrath of God, and only a complete and full repentance, together with a change in the basic values of the nation, can save us. But it is no use even preaching the Gospel at this stage in our history. We are so far advanced on the road of evil that man is being driven faster and faster towards destruction. He is being impelled by forces outside his control and against which he is powerless. What is needed in this country today is the voice of prophecy.

We have to warn mankind of the consequences of the evil forces that have gripped the nation. We have to bring men to *an awareness of God*. Until they have come to the point where they are aware of the presence of God and of his abhorrence of our national way of life, they will not be open to hear the Gospel. A great wall of separation has been erected between man and God. Only the word of God can smash down this wall. Even the Gospel cannot penetrate it, for men will not hear the good news of a saviour for whom they feel no need. Until men come to the point of realization of their need, an awareness of the great danger in which they now stand and the terrible consequences of allowing themselves to continue to be impelled along the path that leads to destruction, they will not be open to hear the Gospel of our Lord and Saviour, they will not be open to the power that can save.

It may well be that men will not hear even the word of prophecy, in which case God will undoubtedly carry out the promise in his word. He has said that he will shake mankind. 'I will *shake* the heavens and the earth and the sea and the dry land; and I will *shake* all nations' (Haggai 2:6). Similarly the writer of Hebrews speaks of the devastation that will follow if we refuse to hear God. 'See that you do not refuse him who is speaking. For if they did not escape when they refused him who warned them on earth, much less shall we escape if we reject him who warns from heaven. His voice then shook the earth; but now he has promised, "Yet once more I will shake not only the earth but also the heaven"' (Hebrews 12:25–26).

Jesus himself foretells times of great trouble and distress that will come upon the nations, times that will herald his own return to the earth. 'And there will be signs in sun and moon and stars, and upon the earth distress of nations in perplexity at the roaring of the sea and the waves, men fainting with fear and with foreboding of what is coming on the world; for the powers of the heavens will be *shaken*. And then they will see the Son of man coming in a cloud with power and great glory. Now when these things begin to take place, look up and raise your heads, because your redemption is drawing near' (Luke 21:25–28).

It may be that today we are living in the times to which Jesus referred, and it may be that he is going to allow not only our own nation and a decadent Europe to continue unabated on the path towards destruction but mankind as a whole to experience devastation on a world scale. There are many indications to support such a belief, but our prime concern in this book is with Britain and with the life of our own nation. Our analysis has revealed what is happening in Britain politically, economically, socially and culturally. The message is clear: Britain is in grave danger. Our nation is being driven by forces that are uncontrollable. Humanly speaking there is no hope of stemming the mounting tidal wave that will sweep our society away into oblivion.

And yet there is hope! The hope is that our nation will hear the word of God and repent before it is too late, before the forces of destruction overwhelm us. Repentance means not simply feeling sorry for ourselves but a realization of the enormity of our crime against God and against mankind, and a determination to turn away from our evil ways and to seek God in penitence and humility. When we turn to him in penitence, as children turning to their father when they know they have done wrong, he will forgive us and restore us to a right relationship both with himself and also with our fellow men and women. It is at this point that we need the Gospel, after the prophetic word of God has brought the nation to penitence. The forces of violence and greed and hatred, that have for so long divided mankind into warring factions and separated man from God, have been broken through the cross of Jesus. But man has to accept him as Saviour in order to share in his victory.

This may be the last chance God is offering to our nation. Certainly the time is short. The forces of destruction are powerfully upon us. The pace at which we are being driven is ever increasing. If we do not hear the word of the Lord, heed his word and repent now, the end is inevitable – it is as inevitable as that day follows night and that night follows day.

(2) *The Weakness of the Church*

This then is the measure of the peril that faces our nation. It is also the measure of the urgency of the task confronting Christians, whose responsibility it is to warn the nation of the consequences of pursuing our present national way of life. Indeed God's indignation will be great upon those who claim to be his people but who do not act as his servants in word and deed, and who do not faithfully bring his word to a rebellious nation in its time of crisis. The responsibility laid upon Christians is enormous, for how shall the nation hear if those who have the word of life are faithless? As Paul puts it, 'But how are men to call upon him in whom they have not believed? And how are they to believe in him of whom they have never heard? And how are they to hear without a preacher?' (Romans 10·14).

The central tragedy of our age is that those forces of social change that we have been noting are reaching their point of ultimate crisis at precisely the point in history when the Church in Britain is weaker than at any time for hundreds of years. All the indications are that we are rapidly reaching the most critical point in the history of mankind since the first coming of Jesus nearly two thousand years ago. Never before has the challenge to Christianity been greater, and yet equally never before has the opportunity for the Gospel been greater.

With the stakes so high it is, of course, inevitable that the

forces of evil at work in our society should challenge the
Christian witness and proclamation of the Gospel as fiercely
as they do today. It is also inevitable that our established
institutions and traditions should be challenged not only in
terms of structure and function but also in terms of their
basic validity. But this in itself is not an unhealthy sign! It
may indeed be the Holy Spirit purging his Church like a
refiner's fire. Only when we emerge cleansed and purified,
and strengthened by the surrounding whole armour of God
shall we be properly armed for the battle and assured of
ultimate victory.

The real danger lies, not in the weakness of the institutional
Church, but in the lack of the authentic voice of prophecy
in our generation. It is the authoritative word of the Lord,
for his people and for the nation in this time of crisis, that
is so desperately needed today. It may well prove to be the
greatest tragedy of history that the Church is unable to rise
to the challenge of today because of the failure of preachers
to speak the word of the Lord with power and authority, and
because of the unwillingness of the people of God to repent
of the extent to which we have allowed the forces of secularization to enter the life of the Church and thereby to
separate us from God. Because, too, of our failure to repent
of the extent to which we have taken things into our own
hands and shut out the power of the Holy Spirit from our
lives.

It may be that the Lord will bypass the institutional
Church. It may be that he has already written ICHABOD
– 'Glory departed' – over our denominations. It may be that
our traditional denominational structures must fall into the
ground and die, in order that the new Church may arise
out of the dust and ashes of the destruction of the old.

It may be that God intends our faithless churches to die
in the destruction that is coming upon the nation. It may be
that those churches that are stuck fast in their traditions, and

are unresponsive to the Holy Spirit, are proving the truth of Jesus' words that it is impossible to put new wine into old wine skins. It may be that what we are seeing is the bursting of the old wine skins – the blowing apart of our traditional religious institutions. It may be that in the devastation that will sweep through our land the Lord will create a new Church out of the faithful remnant.

In Revelation chapter 21 there is a vivid picture of God creating the new city, and the new citizens for the Holy City, and he says, 'Behold, I make *all things* new.' It is worth noting that John's vision of the new city did not include a temple. 'I saw no temple in the city, for its temple is the Lord God the Almighty and the Lamb.' The city had no need of an institutional Church, for the citizens of the Holy City were the temple of the Living God. They had been cleansed and purified and made holy unto the Lord, and his Spirit dwelt within them.

This is a salutary reminder to us that we are not indispensable to God. We Christians who are members of traditional churches will not be allowed to frustrate God's plan of salvation for all the nations, and his purpose in creation and re-creation, that are being unfolded on the stage of human history in a mighty way in our own life and times. We need to be reminded that God can reject us and raise up servants to himself from the stones of the ground, if he so chooses.

There are already many indications that the Lord is calling people out from dead traditional churches to form new fellowships that are open to the power of the Holy Spirit. God is certainly doing a new thing in our day. There is, of course, danger in this. There is danger in all new movements, even spiritual movements, unless they are soundly rooted in basic truth. Yet it is only through the constant challenge to tradition and the willingness to embrace change that growth occurs. The history of the Christian Church is a record of schism, of fission and fusion, of the re-emphasis of some neglected part of God's truth that speaks to the changing needs of man in each new age. Those who challenge tradition are always regarded as dangerous fanatics, by the conservatives who are dedicated to preserving the *status quo* against the invasion of anything new. The traditionalists play a valuable part in providing stability in times of radical change, yet they stand in danger of resisting the Holy Spirit in times when God is injecting new creativity into a dead society and calling his people to the boldness of a new venture in the power of his Spirit.

We are in such a situation today, when our nation is facing its social and moral Dunkirk, when we lack the moral fibre to counter the economic forces that are engulfing us, when 'the family' as the core institution in our society is beginning to disintegrate. What is most needed today is for Christians to give a bold lead to the nation, to point the way to the re-establishment of the social foundations of Britain firmly resting upon a spiritual basis in a new relationship with God through the Lordship of Jesus.

In order to give this spiritual lead to the nation there are two paramount issues that Christians have to face. The first is a need for a new openness to the Holy Spirit, and the second is the need for a prophetic ministry. We must look briefly at these two needs.

(a) The Need for Openness to the Holy Spirit

The Spirit, as Jesus said, is like the wind – you can feel it and even hear it, but you don't know where it has come from or where it is going to. In the same way you can feel and experience the power of the Holy Spirit blowing through our land today. At the moment it is like a faint breeze that gently disturbs the calm of a summer afternoon, but the day is coming when it will blow like a whirlwind through the land, sweeping away all that is not holy in the life of the Church and of the nation, and breaking down the barriers that resist the power of his coming.

There are many Christians who long to see God at work in our land and who pray for his coming, but they do not realize just what they are asking. As Amos warned, 'Woe to you who desire the day of the Lord! Why would you have the day of the Lord? It is darkness, and not light; as if a man fled from a lion, and a bear met him; or went into the house and leaned with his hand against the wall, and a serpent bit him. Is not the day of the Lord darkness, and not light, and gloom with no brightness in it?' (Amos 5:18–20). The prophet went on to declare that God hated all the trappings of religion that abounded in the nation but were not accompanied by righteous living. 'Let justice roll down like waters, and righteousness like an ever-flowing stream' (v. 24).

Similarly, Malachi warns that when God acts in the life of the nation, or on a worldwide scale, it will not be a comfortable time for anyone. 'The Lord whom you seek will suddenly come ... But who can endure the day of his coming, and who can stand when he appears? For he is like a refiner's fire . a refiner and purifier of silver' (Malachi 3:1–3).

Salvation and renewal must begin at the household of God, with Christ's own people. It is *we* who have to come in penitence before the Lord, confessing our own powerlessness and failure. Every attempt to resuscitate the life of the Church is doomed to failure unless it is born of the Holy Spirit. Our pathetic attempts at structural reform, at increasing the efficiency of our organizations, and at engineering ecumenical unity schemes cannot succeed unless they are directed by the Spirit. Evangelism and spiritual growth are not things that we can plan and direct with our human wisdom and creative abilities. However much we invest our human energies into campaigns, crusades and programmes of growth and outreach, all is a waste of time and a use-less expenditure of energy unless we ourselves are under the authority and direction of the Holy Spirit. 'Unless the Lord builds the house, those who build it labour in vain' (Psalm 127:1). Energetic Christian builders and planners, and ecumenical activists, have never really heeded this warning. The ecclesiastical bureaucrats will go on directing the denominations regardless of the consequences!

But the day of reckoning for the Church cannot be long delayed. If our traditional churches and denominations are dead we should have the faith to bury them! There are limits to the effectiveness of artificial respiration. It is no use massaging a corpse! Only the God of the resurrection can put new life into the dead. That is the only hope for churches stuck in the deadness of tradition. But it may be that the Lord is showing us the utter irrelevance of our traditional churches in the new creation that he is about to bring into being. Instead of being afraid of the massive changes that are taking place in our generation, we should be concerned with one major objective, and that is, to be open to the power and direction of the Holy Spirit so that the God of creation may be able to use us.

This, in fact, was God's original purpose in bringing the Church into being. He planned, before the beginning of Creation, to use the Church in the cosmic battle against the forces of evil. Paul looks forward to the time when 'through the church the manifold wisdom of God might now be made known to the principalities and powers in the heavenly places' (Ephesians 3:10). God's purpose is to use those of his own people who are open to the power of his Spirit, to cleanse and perfect them and to fill them with his strength in order to arm them for the battle – the climax of the ages – to defeat the primeval enemy of mankind. God is offering to Christians in our generation the most incredible privilege – that of being used by him in one of the most crucial periods in the history of mankind.

This is a day of immense opportunity as well as of challenge, but Christians must beware of accepting the challenge in their own strength or it will overwhelm them. If we are able rightly to discern the signs of the times, the Lord is already moving up and down our land in a creative movement of the Holy Spirit. The institutional weakness of the Church will not hinder this movement. Indeed, it offers to Christians a great opportunity for spiritual growth, for it is in the times of the greatest realization of our weakness that the Lord can do most with us and through us. It may be that on the anvil of our weakness the Lord is hammering out the matrix of his new Church. 'My grace is sufficient for you, for my power is made perfect in weakness' (2 Corinthians 12:9). This was Paul's experience of the way God used his own weakness to pour in the power and strength of the Holy Spirit.

Our confession of powerlessness is the prerequisite for the filling of the Holy Spirit, just as our confession of failure and sinfulness is the prerequisite of forgiveness and salvation. The time has come! The Lord is at hand! We shall see God doing mighty things in our generation. He chooses the time – we do not. He chose the time of his incarnation when the Word was made flesh, and he has 'a plan for the fullness of time' (Ephesians 1:10), which he began in Christ and which he is continuing to unfold before the nations in our generation. He plans to use us in his plan of re-creation. His plans for us are 'for welfare and not for evil, to give you a future and a hope' (Jeremiah 29:11).

The time has come for the people of God to awaken out of their slumbers! The night is nearly over. The day is at hand. It is time to arise out of the syndrome of failure and depression, to shake off the cobwebs of inertia, to put aside our fears and frustrations, and to put our trust in the Lord.

We need to trust him, with all the simplicity and faith of Abraham leaving the old familiar country and going out into the unknown to witness the fulfilment of God's promise to create a new people in a new land.

(b) *The Need for a Prophetic Ministry*

The time of revival is at hand! The times of refreshment promised in scripture are coming upon us (Acts 3:19). Now is the time for a new boldness among the people of God, for a new prophetic proclamation of the word of God, that will prepare the way for a great new evangelistic movement. God is giving to our nation an opportunity to enter into the most glorious period in her history, when she can truly become the servant of the Lord, but first there has to be repentance and a turning away from the decadence and wickedness that at present characterize her life. The task that the Lord is laying upon his true people – all who will be obedient to his word and who are alive in his Spirit – is to act as his mouthpiece to the nation, to reveal his purpose to the people.

The prophetic proclamation of the word of the Lord has to come first. It is fruitless preaching the Gospel to a decadent nation that is so far steeped in its wicked and sinful ways that it is not open to receiving it. People do not want to hear good news if they do not feel they have any need of it. It is no use telling them that Jesus is their Saviour if they have no awareness of their need for a saviour. The awareness of need comes through an awareness of the situation, and an appreciation of the danger confronting our nation and an understanding of the times in which we live. That is the prophetic task to which the Lord is calling his people. It is the basic task of proclaiming his word, that he is God, and that there is no other, that he is a God of righteousness, truth and justice. Man is the child of his creation and we cannot disobey his fundamental laws without suffering the consequences.

The forces of evil that are driving our nation towards destruction are also driving our world towards annihilation. They are threatening to destroy the whole of God's created order in our world. God cannot tolerate this, there is a limit to which he can allow the wickedness of man to have free reign. If our nation turned to God now the Lord could use us in a mighty way in the restoration of mankind and the establishment of an age of righteousness and justice world-wide. But first our own nation has to hear and to heed the word of God, and to come under his authority and the Lordship of Jesus.

The prophetic task to which God is calling his people in Britain today is not simply the task of a single prophet or of the professional preachers, but of all God's people, all who love the Lord Jesus Christ. Moses said, 'I wish that the Lord would give his spirit to all his people and make all of them shout like prophets' (Numbers 11:29; G.N.B.). When we understand what is happening to our nation and how we are being driven by forces outside human control, then we realize our need for God and we realize also the urgency of proclaiming his word in the ears of the nation. It is only when as a nation we become aware of the dangers threatening to overwhelm us that there will be an openness to the Gospel, a willingness to turn to the Lord and to hear his word and seek his way. It is the prophetic proclamation of the word of the Lord that creates that hunger for the Gospel that lays the foundation for an evangelistic movement.

Once Christians themselves are alerted to the dangers facing our nation, they will begin to witness in a prophetic manner to their friends and neighbours and within their own families.

There can be no doubt that such a commitment to a prophetic mission in the life of our nation would transform and renew our churches. It would bring a new spiritual dimension and a new experience of the power and presence of the risen Lord in our midst. However fearfully we undertook the task of speaking prophetically to our neighbours, our experience would be like that of 'the seventy' who returned rejoicing in their new-found experience of power, that even the evil spirits were subject to them. Such an experience opens us up to God in a new way, so that his power can really take control. The experience is in itself infectious – it communicates to others without the contrived efficacy of planned strategy. This is the way that a national movement of spiritual revival will build up, through the personal experience of the presence and power of the risen Lord in an ever-growing number of individual lives. This is what happened amongst first-century Christians.

A spirit of praise dominated the fellowship, life and worship of the early Church. For the believers in the New Testament times, church worship was a coming together 'to share their joy in the Lord' and to recount to one another all the wonderful things the Lord had done since last they met. The dynamic power of the Holy Spirit moved mightily amongst them in their daily lives, and when they came together for worship they could not keep quiet, they were filled with praise and the knowledge of the presence of the living Christ. When Christians experience the joy of being used by Christ as his witnesses in their daily lives, the regular worship of the church is transformed and revitalized by a fresh experience of the presence of Jesus and by a new spirit of praise and adoration. It may be that when this happens the differences in belief and tradition, that have for so long divided the Church, will become of less and less significance. Perhaps an unexpected by-product of the period of spiritual renewal to which God is pointing us will be the production of a new basis of unity amongst the churches. It will be a unity that is rooted and grounded in the experience of being 'in Christ', and born out of obedience and trust in the power of the risen Jesus.

But the hope of restoration which the Lord is offering to our nation depends upon our hearing and heeding his word and turning to him in penitence. In the same way, the hope of renewal for the Church depends upon the faithfulness of the people of Christ and their openness and obedience to the Holy Spirit. Christians have to warn the nation of the dangers facing it, but the message we have to proclaim is not simply one of doom and judgement, it is also a message of God's love and forgiveness, of his Fatherly care for the whole family of mankind. It is not the Father's wish that even one should be lost. It is his wish that all should be saved and should know him as Father. Ours is the task to proclaim the truth about God and to point to the way of salvation through Jesus Christ. The dangers facing our nation are enormous, but so too is the opportunity to build a new nation living a new way of life as the people of God and under his power and authority. Through trust in God Britain can reach new heights of glory in his service in our world.

God is holding out before our nation the prospect of a wonderful new period in our history, a time of restoration, of peace and love and unity – a time of living in the power of his Spirit. But the conditions of entering into such a period of peace and plenty, and experiencing all the mighty blessings of God, are those of repentance and turning from our wicked ways. But – **our nation has first to hear and to heed the word of God. If we do not the forces of destruction that are already well advanced will continue on their way.** The Lord will not save us. The sons of disobedience will suffer the inevitable consequences of their evil ways.

Christians have to offer men the choice between good and evil. They have to proclaim God's judgement on the old order whilst pointing to the new one. We have to tell of God's judgement upon mankind's wicked ways and at the same time speak and witness to his love and the forgiveness he offers through the Lord Jesus Christ. This is the measure of the prophetic task that is being laid upon Christians. If the word of the Lord is not heard and heeded the results will be so terrible as to defy description. If the word of the Lord is heeded there are wonderful times ahead. **God is giving to Christians the immense privilege of being fundamentally involved in a new creative period in the history of mankind.** It will be a time for the re-assessment of the moral basis of our national life. It will be a time for looking again at the basic structures of our society and for re-examining the fundamental values upon which they are founded.

Many of the great issues affecting our national life require social programmes and political action if there are to be any fundamental changes. This does not mean that the Gospel provides a political platform or a ready-made programme of social reform. It is in the realm of basic values that the Gospel has a creative part to play. The paramount duty laid upon Christians today is to proclaim the truth about man, about society and about God.

In particular, Christians have to make known the good news that God has provided for all the needs of mankind, both individual and corporate. It is for this good news that there is such a great yearning in the nation today. Men and women and young people are looking for authoritative answers to the problems that confront them in their personal lives and in the social life of the nation. Christians need to feel the excitement of the assurance that they have this good news to offer. We are like the four lepers who went to the enemy camp to beg food when the Syrians were laying siege to the capital city of ancient Israel, and found the camp deserted. A rumour had spread panic amongst the enemy and they had fled in disarray back to their own borders, leaving the camp filled with food and booty, the spoils of war, and strewing the countryside with cast-off weapons as they fled in confusion. The four hungry lepers filled themselves with food and then they remembered the starving people in the city who still thought they were prisoners. Every hour's delay meant that more people would die. One said to the others, 'This day is a day of good news and we are keeping silent. We must go back to the city and tell the people they are free and that there is food and drink for all' (see 2 Kings 7:9). Christians today have a similar task to proclaim the good news to the people of Britain, the good news that they can be free from bondage to the forces of evil which have gripped the life of the nation and are driving it relentlessly towards destruction. We are set free through what God has done through Christ.

For those who have eyes to see and ears to hear and minds to understand the signs of the times, the message is clear. God is already at work in our land, renewing and revitalizing the lives of those who are open to him. At the moment the renewing work of the Holy Spirit is but a small stream rippling through the country, but it is growing steadily and the day will come when it becomes a mighty river flowing through the land, bringing cleansing and renewal to all people – to all who will hear and receive the good news.

Every Christian is needed to share in the massive task of bringing Christ to our nation, where the majority of people lack even an awareness of God. We can no longer afford to leave it to the professional preachers and evangelists. The task is urgent! As in the New Testament, where every Christian was a witness, so today everyone who has committed his or her life to Jesus is needed to be a witness to his truth, to proclaim the word of the Lord to their neighbours.

Not everyone has the gift of prophetic insight, but all can share in the prophetic ministry to the nation. All Christians who are alive in Christ, and thus open to God's Spirit, can discern the authentic voice of that Spirit. The Spirit himself bears witness within us. We know immediately and intuitively when we are in the presence of the Spirit, and when we hear the authentic voice of God. The Spirit who gives life within us prompts us to know the Truth when we encounter it. As the unborn John the Baptist leapt within his mother's womb when she came into the presence of the Lord Jesus, so the Spirit within us bears testimony to his presence in others.

The urgency of the task confronting us demands the mobilization of the total resources of the Body of Christ to share in the ministry of prophecy to the nation. As a nation we have for many years been living upon the spiritual reserves invested by former generations. But just as in economic matters our bank balance becomes exhausted if it is not replenished, so in spiritual matters our spiritual reserves become drained. We are at present in a period such as that foretold by the prophet Amos, ' "Behold, the days are coming," says the Lord God, "when I will send a famine on the land; not a famine of bread, nor a thirst for water, but of hearing the words of the Lord"' (Amos 8:11).

The days of famine are almost at an end. The word of the Lord will again be heard in our land with clarity, power and authority! God has already provided for that day, just as he has provided the answers to all man's needs in Jesus Christ. He says, 'If my people who are called by my name humble themselves, and pray and seek my face, and turn from their wicked ways, then I will hear from heaven, and will forgive their sin and heal their land' (2 Chronicles 7:14).

Will the Christians rise to their prophetic task? Will the nation hear the word of the Lord and repent? Will God intervene to stem the forces of destruction that are gathering momentum in our land? Will the Day of the Lord be a day of darkness or of light?

It may be that God intends taking us through a period of suffering. Maybe the Church will be going underground within the next few years. Maybe 1984 is not just a fiction-writer's dream! Perhaps we are being prepared now for a period of persecution such as the Church in the West has never known in modern times. Maybe the world is soon to plunge into the most devastating war in the history of mankind.

The time is short! The night is far spent! The day is at hand! What will the dawn bring forth? Will it be a day of darkness or of light? We do not have long to wait for the answer to these questions.

NOTES

1. Robinson, T. H., *Prophecy and the Prophets in Ancient Israel*, Duckworth, London, 1968; chapters 3 and 4.
2. Marx, Karl, *Critique of Political Economy*, Lawrence & Wishart, London, 1940; p. 13.
3. Malinowski, B., *A Scientific Theory of Culture*, Oxford University Press, 1960.
4. Malinowski, B., *The Dynamics of Culture Change*, Yale University Press, New Haven, Connecticut, 1945.
5. Parsons, Talcott, *The Social System*, Tavistock Press, London, 1952; p. 5.
6. Beeson, Trevor, *Britain Today and Tomorrow*, Fount Paperbacks, London, 1978.
7. See Marx's essay on 'Alienation' in *Marxist Leninist Library*, 20 vols, Lawrence & Wishart, London, 1936–40.
8. Marx, Karl, *Economic & Philosophic MSS of 1845*, Lawrence & Wishart, London, 1940.
9. Parsons, Talcott, *Essays in Sociological Theory*, Glencoe Free Press, Glencoe, Illinois, 1954.
10. Parsons, Talcott, 'Pattern Variables Revisited: A Response to Robert Dubin', *American Sociological Review* 1960; vol. 25, pp. 467–83.
11. Parsons, Talcott, *Structure and Process in Modern Societies*, Glencoe Free Press, Glencoe, Illinois, 1959; p. 172.
12. Parsons, Talcott, *et al.*, *Theories of Society*, 2 vols, Glencoe Free Press, Glencoe, Illinois, 1961.
13. Weber, Max, *The Protestant Ethic and the Spirit of Capitalism* (first published in English, translated by T. Parsons), Allen & Unwin, London, 1931.
14. Robertson, H. M., *Aspects of the Rise of Economic Individualism*, Cambridge University Press, 1933.
15. Fanfani, A., *Catholicism, Protestantism and Capitalism*, Allen & Unwin, London, 1935.
16. Samuelson, K., *Religious & Economic Action*, London, 1955.

17. Andreski, Stanislav, 'Method and Substantive Theory in Max Weber', *British Journal of Sociology*, December 1964; pp. 8f.

18. Eisenstadt, S. N., 'The Protestant Ethic Thesis' in *The Sociology of Religion*, Robertson R., ed., Penguin, London, 1969; p. 310.

19. ibid., p. 310.

20. Marx, Karl and Engels, Frederick, *Manifesto of the Communist Party*, Lawrence & Wishart, London, 1938; p. 20.

21. Pearce, A., Cross Section, Box BM. 4226, London WC1V 6XX.

22. In a depressing survey of the decline of Christianity in the West, David Edwards sees in the renewal movement the one ray of hope. Cf. Edwards, David L., *Religion and Change*, Hodder & Stoughton, London, 1974; p. 278.

23. Cox, Harvey, *The Secular City*, Pelican, London, 1968.